OUR STORY BEGINS

YOUR FAVORITE AUTHORS AND ILLUSTRATORS
SHARE FUN, INSPIRING, AND
OCCASIONALLY RIDICULOUS THINGS
THEY WROTE AND DREW AS KIDS

Atheneum Books for Young Readers

New York   London   Toronto   Sydney   New Delhi

ATHENEUM BOOKS FOR YOUNG READERS
An imprint of Simon & Schuster Children's Publishing Division
1230 Avenue of the Americas, New York, New York 10020

To every kid with a story inside, and to all
the grown-ups who give them a pencil and
encourage them to begin

—E. B. W.

The Writer's Dream

I hold dreams of writing
Deep inside my heart.
I want to touch people's emotions
Using this expressive art.
I wish to stimulate contemplation
Of the joy which can partner life,
To diffuse the sorrow of others,
And help them through any strife.
This now shall be my purpose
And a crucially important goal.
For I attempt to return happiness to the spirit
And contentment to the soul.

—CYNTHIA LEITICH SMITH, age 11
(page 93)

[CONTENTS]

OUR
STORY
BEGINS

OUR STORY BEGINS with a box in a basement. It's brown and heavy and one of many marked *Elissa*. And it's filled, to the brim, with stories from my childhood. Stories I wrote.

Going through the box is like going backward in time. The stories on top of the pile are long and typed; they're stapled pages from an ink-jet printer, with chapter titles in funky fonts. Below that are notebooks (spiral-bound, then marble-covered), then loose pages of text I once hammered out on my dad's typewriter. At the very bottom are ruled lines on yellowed paper, my six-year-old handwriting large and exact. Some stories in the box made me laugh, they were so clever. Others made me laugh because they were so bad. Is it any surprise I became a writer?

I knew I couldn't be the only one with a box in a basement. What, I wondered, did other children's authors write when they were their readers' age? Illustrators, too. What did they draw? I couldn't be the only one who'd want to know. So I began to ask.

Over the past two years, I've had the joy of talking to some of today's most-beloved children's authors and illustrators about their early artistic endeavors. This book contains just a small sample of that childhood creativity. Some now-famous authors didn't write as kids. Some wrote or drew, but they didn't save their work. Others saved but consider their work too personal to share. Some were too busy creating something new to dig out something old. And, unfortunately, I had the space to include only a fraction of today's tremendous talent.

Even so, the collection you're about to read contains a fascinating variety of work from a range of voices, styles, backgrounds, and experiences, arranged by the age at which the works were created, from seven up through sixteen. Phyllis Reynolds Naylor wrote mysteries on used stationery during the Great Depression. Tom Angleberger planned for an epic novel about a plaice called Yodium. Rita Williams-Garcia kept a daily chronicle of her offbeat elementary school life. Thanhhà Lại made up stories with her mother as a girl in Vietnam, while Yuyi Morales struggled to create a truly original painting as a young teen in Mexico. These are just a few of this book's poems, comics, journal entries, stories, drawings, paintings, and speeches, from different genres, different places, and different decades.

More amazing than the differences, though, are the similarities. Every piece is bursting with imagination and personality. The writing is sweet and funny and peppered with errors. The art is bold and uninhibited, with visible eraser marks. The whole collection is honest and passionate and often over-the-top. It's *raw*, in every sense of the word. It reflects the authors and artists these authors and artists admired, and, without a doubt, the authors and artists they'd someday become.

Everyone's story begins somewhere. For these writers and illustrators, it began with a favorite book or the sound of a poem. With dreams about horses, or Broadway, or monsters, or adventure. With parents who read aloud, or spoke poetically, or praised their creativity. It began with teachers— they remember their names—who transcribed their ideas, or laughed at their jokes, or wrote *You will make your living as a writer someday* in the margin with red pen.

Someday, the people in this book would win Newberys and Caldecotts. They'd top bestseller lists and see their books made into feature films. They'd inspire millions of kids to read, write, draw, and dream.

But long before that, they were kids themselves. Their stories were just beginning.

Your story is beginning too. Where will it go?

—E. B. W.

1

[Dan Santat]

I REMEMBER SEEING my first Norman Rockwell painting when I was five. It was a picture of a snowy cottage in an issue of *Time* magazine. I was amazed by how detailed and realistic it looked, and it was at that moment right there that I concluded this man was the greatest artist who ever lived. It was as if someone had created life with their hands.

That evening, I set myself up at my usual drawing spot in front of the TV set, pulled out my markers and crayons, and tried to copy the picture as best as I could. I loved to draw, and I remember thinking that the whole town would be in awe of my artistic skills once I had replicated this masterpiece. News reporters would come from miles around to do a story on me with a headline reading, "Genius Child Paints Exactly Like Norman Rockwell!"

After an hour of drawing with my crayons, I became frustrated and started to cry. My dad laughed and said, "Norman Rockwell painted for years. It takes years of practice and talent to be that good."

The thought of *not* being able to draw something made me furious. I slowly flipped through the entire Norman Rockwell art book. Each painting taunted me as I stared longingly at its individual beauty. Each one whispered, "You will never be able to do this."

The worst part was that the book concluded with an image of Norman Rockwell painting an exact portrait of himself.

It was the ultimate slap in the face.

But I noticed something else about that painting.

Norman Rockwell was old. My five-year-old judgment of age concluded that he was probably a thousand years old. I remembered how, earlier that evening, my dad had mentioned that Norman Rockwell had painted for years to become that good.

NORMAN ROCKWELL HAD A THOUSAND YEARS OF PRACTICE ON ME.

And I was only five.

So I began to draw. I practiced every day, copying pictures from all sorts of cool comics like *Peanuts* and *Garfield* from the newspapers, and the *Smurfs* and *Flintstones* from the cartoons. I quickly improved after each drawing. I could feel my powers growing, and news of my ability to draw spread quickly around my school. (It wasn't the whole town, but it was a start.)

"Could you draw me a Pegasus?" a kid would ask.

"Can you draw a knight fighting a dragon?" asked another.

I would fill their requests for a quarter, but I also drew their pictures just so I would know that I was capable of making whatever it was that a person wanted.

I hated knowing that I couldn't draw something.

As I grew older, I gave myself tougher challenges. In high school, I copied pictures of Spider-Man, the Incredible Hulk,

by Dan Santat, age 7

and the X-Men. I wanted to figure out how muscles and bones worked, so I checked out books on how to draw and slowly increased my knowledge. No one pushed me to draw; I wanted to improve on my own. I was passionate about art.

Years later, in college, I was taking a biology class and studying the human cell. My friend looked over at my notes and was astonished at the detailed drawing of the cell that I had drawn in my notebook.

"Dude, that is the most amazing Golgi apparatus I have ever seen!"

I smiled.

"Why are you even here? Why aren't you in art school?" my friend asked.

by **Dan Santat**, age **10**

"My parents want me to be a doctor," I replied.

"But you stink at biology, and it's totally obvious you love to draw."

His comment made me think long and hard. Was I making a mistake by not doing art for a living?

Suddenly, I saw an image from the corner of my eye, and it was as if fate had struck me square in the face.

On the cover of one of our biology handouts was a Xeroxed image of a doctor taking care of a little girl's doll, painted by none other than that thousand-year-old man, NORMAN ROCKWELL!

He was still mocking me, after all these years. "You will never be able to do this."

So I applied to art school, and now, I make books for children.

Thirty-five years after seeing my first Norman Rockwell painting, I still can't paint as well as the man . . .

But I know I still have another 960 years to go.

Dan Santat is an author and illustrator of books for children. He is the 2015 Caldecott medalist for *The Adventures of Beekle: The Unimaginary Friend* and won a silver medal in illustration from the Society of Illustrators for *Oh No! (Or How My Science Project Destroyed the World)*, written by Mac Barnett. He is also the creator of the Disney animated series *The Replacements*. Visit him at dantat.com.

2

[R. J. Palacio]

I **ALWAYS KNEW** I wanted be a writer and an artist. The two went hand in hand for me. Even if the assignment was to write a poem, I would draw a picture to accompany it. My teachers always encouraged my drawings and told my mother I had "talent."

Both my parents were passionate book lovers, so I grew up in a home full of books. My mother's favorite "children's" book to read to me at night was *The Little Prince*. That, and the short stories of Oscar Wilde. My father was a gifted storyteller, who would tell me stories about the constellations and planets. Both of them, my mom and my dad, always supported my drawing and writing. They acted like everything I ever created was a masterpiece, and, strangely enough, I believed them. The confidence boost you get from that kind of unconditional love—the sense that your creative efforts have true value—really does stay with you forever. As does the notion, which I inherited from my parents, that growing up to be an artist or a writer is just about the greatest thing a person can become in life, the highest kind of achievement.

I had a few recurring obsessions, even back then, that have stayed with me as a grown-up. I've always loved horses. I used to draw them all the time, in the margins of my notebooks, on the blue denim cover of my loose-leaf binder. And I always loved Greek mythology: stories of the gods and goddesses of Olympus, the fantastical creatures. The story of Pegasus was the perfect convergence of my two passions— horses and Greek myths. The poem "Winged Steed" was published in the school newspaper when I was in the third grade. It was the first piece of my writing that ever got published, and I remember feeling completely elated that people would be reading *my* words, *my* feelings. Reading it now, I doubt I even knew what half the words meant, but I liked that kind of flowery language at the time. I had made an accompanying drawing, which they didn't publish, so I'm glad to have the opportunity now, after all these years, to finally see it in print!

I still fill my notebooks with doodles of horses, by the way. And I still dream of winged steeds.

by R. J. Palacio, age 8

```
       Winged Steed
Oh, beautiful winged steed,
Black as night with wings white as
   pearl,
Give me your grace which is oh!
   so lovely.
Horse among horse, beyond immortal,
Fly faster than wind and higher above.
Twilight your eyes, but gentle you are,
With a frenzy above mortality.
The gift of flight is bestowed upon you,
   with everlasting life,
But gentle you are, winged steed, with
   strength, endurance and strife.
Graceful you fly along the endless
   cloudless sky.
Please remember in your dreams for,
I will remember you.
       Raquel Jaramillo
```

R. J. Palacio's debut novel was the number-one *New York Times* bestselling *Wonder*, which has sold over five million copies worldwide since its publication in 2012. The book is about a ten-year-old named Auggie Pullman, a boy who was born with a rare craniofacial difference, and the circle of people around him as he enters school for the first time in the fifth grade. *Wonder*'s message of tolerance and inclusion launched the Choose Kind movement, which has been embraced by numerous media outlets, including *Good Morning America, LIVE! with Kelly*, the *Wall Street Journal, Entertainment Weekly*, and more. She is also the author of *365 Days of Wonder: Mr. Browne's Book of Precepts*, and *Auggie & Me: Three Wonder Stories*, which includes the novellas *The Julian Chapter, Pluto*, and *Shingaling. Wonder* is being adapted for the big screen by Lionsgate in a movie starring Julia Roberts and Owen Wilson. R. J. Palacio resides in New York City with her husband, two sons, and two dogs. Visit her online at rjpalacio.com.

3

[Marla Frazee]

WHEN I WAS A KID, I made a lot of small, crayoned, stapled-together books. Some look as though I tossed them off in a few minutes. Others seem as if I spent some time on them. But from as far back as I can remember, I've always wanted to become a children's book author and illustrator. I think this is mainly because there were certain books that I loved so deeply. My favorites were *The Carrot Seed*, *Blueberries for Sal*, and *Where the Wild Things Are*. I loved reading about Henry and Ribsy and Beezus and Ramona, because, well, who doesn't? I pored over *Peanuts* cartoons. I got pretty good at drawing Snoopy, and I drew him on whatever piece of paper I could find, over and over and over again.

When I was in the third grade, I embarked on my own chapter book series called June and John. As it turned out, I only got as far as one book in the series, and it has just three chapters. "June and John" is the first. The second chapter is "The Beach." The third chapter is "The Only Apple." That's it! I guess I had other important things to do. (Like breaking the world record for the most pogo-stick jumps without falling. Which I did! But Guinness World Records wrote a letter saying that since only kids were witnesses to the event, it wasn't official.)

You will see that June and John live on a street with a name very close to Beverly Cleary's Klickitat Street. As for their dog, I just named him Snoopy. Copying our first mentors is an excellent way to find our own voice as authors and illustrators, or maybe I just believe that because that's what I did.

I drew the illustrations on the stationery my dad brought home from work—the letterhead shows through the back side. And I'm not sure who made the corrections in the text. A teacher? My mom?

At any rate, here's chapter 1 about June and John.

Marla Frazee was awarded a Caldecott Honor for *All the World* and *A Couple of Boys Have the Best Week Ever* and the *Boston Globe–Horn Book* Award for Picture Books for her wordless book *The Farmer and the Clown*. She is the author-illustrator of *Roller Coaster*, *Walk On!*, *Santa Claus the World's*

CONTINUED ON PAGE 23

June and John

    June and John ~~are~~ _were_ twins. They ~~are~~ _were_ in the second grade, so they ~~are~~ _were_ 7 _seven_ years old. They lived in a white house on Klickit St. They ~~also~~ had a dog named "Snoopy."

June was feeding Snoopy, while John came with a big piece of paper and a paint brush. June got up, and looked at him with a puzzled look.

"What in the world are you going to do?" she said after a moment's hesitation.

"I'm going to sell lemonade" he said. "This is a paper for my sign. Will you come and help me get the green paint?"

"Yes, I guess so," she answered.

They walked to the garage. John got the ladder and leaned it against the wall. "Now hold it still", he said.

"Okay."

John climbed the ladder, and reached for the paint. He found the paint
and started down the ladder. Then Snoopy

came up behind the ladder, and started
barking at John. Snoopy scared John,
and John dropped the paint. The paint
fell and burst open! June's shoes that
were white were now green, and Snoopy
that was black and white was now

all green." We'd better clean my shoes,"
yelled June who didn't care how green
Snoopy was.

"We'd better clean Snoopy," said John
who didn't care how green June's shoes
were.

They both ran to get a rag. But
by the time they found the rags the
paint had dried! "Oh dear," said June, "We'd
better get terpintine!"
                turpentine

"Sorry to say," said John, "We don't
have any!"

They both went into the house,
and June was running around in her
socks looking for some soap, and John
was running around trying to find something big enough to hold Snoopy. June
found her soap, and soaked her shoes
in the bathroom sink. When the paint
came off, she went to help John who
had put Snoopy in the bathtub. He was
having trouble, but after an hour and
a half he got the dog clean.

"Now let's get crayons and make our sign", said John who was relieved to have the paint cleaned up.

"Okay", said June, "We can earn money for the paint by selling lemonade."

......And that is what they did. You may be happy to know that they made the lemonade without spilling it all over!

Number One Toy Expert, *Boot & Shoe*, *The Boss Baby* (which inspired the DreamWorks Animation movie *The Boss Baby*), and *The Bossier Baby*, as well as the illustrator of many other books, including *The Seven Silly Eaters*, *Stars*, the *New York Times* bestselling Clementine series, and *God Got a Dog*. Marla has three grown sons and works in a small backyard cabin under an avocado tree. Visit her online at marlafrazee.com.

4

[Jarrett J. Krosoczka]

I WAS IN THE THIRD GRADE when I wrote my first book. We were studying Greek mythology, and our teacher instructed us to invent a creation story. I wrote a tale of an owl that cheated Hermes out of a win—and was turned into the moon. This school project ignited a fire within me. I had always liked to draw, and I always loved characters—but this was the first time it all came together in a book for me. I remember our teacher introducing us to the concept of "brainstorming," organizing our ideas, laying out the book, revising, and then moving to the finished draft. I use all of these tools today in the books that I write and illustrate that get published.

But published or not, an author is somebody who writes a

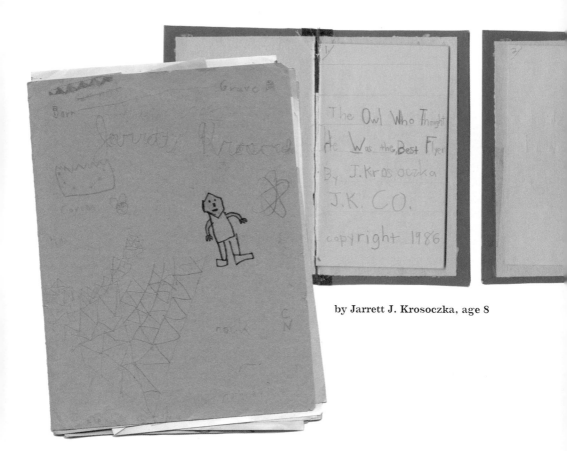

by Jarrett J. Krosoczka, age 8

book. So do you know what that means? I became an author in the third grade! My literary efforts weren't confined to just school hours. I couldn't wait to get home and write and draw. I'd make my own books and my own comics every day after school and on the weekends. I loved passing these papers around to my friends and watching them take enjoyment out of my tales. So what I do now for my job is exactly what I did for fun when I was a kid.

There was once an owl who thought he was the best flyer. He wanted to have a challenge with Hermes.

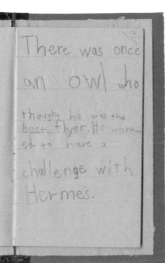

Once he flew over to Mount Olympus.

He watched Hermes until dark so he would know where Hermes would be.

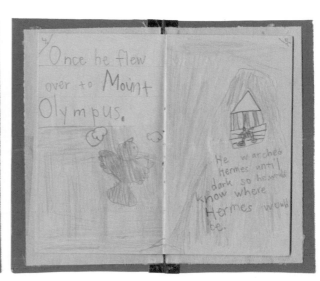

When the owl went back to his tree he started to practice stunt flying. He planned to ask Hermes for a challenge the next day.

When the owl asked Hermes, he agreed.

yes

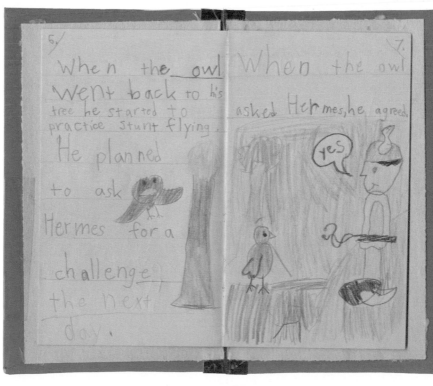

8/ But when the
owl made a course
he made a short cut.
So the owl said "The
one who wins
could do anything
to the other."

9/ So they had
the flying
contest.

10/

11/

Jarrett J. Krosoczka is the author and/or illustrator of more than thirty published books. His titles include picture books (*Punk Farm*), novels (*Platypus Police Squad: The Frog Who Croaked*), and graphic novels (*Lunch Lady and the Cyborg Substitute*). He's delivered two TED Talks, which have amassed more than two million views online, and he can be heard weekly on SiriusXM's *Kids Place Live* during his book segment. Visit Jarrett online at studiojjk.com.

5

[Thanhhà Lại]

I **DON'T HAVE ANYTHING SAVED** from my childhood except for some family photographs and the first-grade school picture shown. Everything else—drawings, writings, report cards, baby clothes, embroideries—was abandoned in Vietnam. My family and I left in a panic two days before the war ended in 1975. I was ten. After forty years, I'm certain those artifacts have turned to dust. So I have nothing to show you in terms of concrete evidence of the beginning of a writer. But it turns out, I don't need tangible objects. I have my memories.

I remember spending hours upon hours listening to my mother tell stories of her childhood. Somewhere in the midst of listening, I began to invent stories for her. We usually shared time before bed, inside a mosquito net, with an electric fan on low blowing a tropical warmth away from us.

We spoke in Vietnamese, a language that is naturally poetic and rhythmic. My mother was a house poet, meaning she recited and created poems for inside the house, never seeking notice from the outside. That was how she was raised. I listened for years, and somewhere along the way, the cadences and images within her words sank into my marrow. When I think in Vietnamese, I can't help but process the sentences as poems.

Here's a story I told my mom when I was maybe eight, in a much more humble Vietnamese than hers. I'm writing it in a prose poem to convey how the words lined up in my Vietnamese mind. I asked my mom recently if she remembers this story about a bird in a cage, and yes, she does indeed.

Thanhhà Lại was born in Vietnam and now lives north of New York City. She wrote *Inside Out and Back Again*, which won a National Book Award for Children's Literature and a Newbery Honor, and *Listen, Slowly*, a *New York Times* bestseller. Visit Thanhhà online at thanhhalai.com.

by Thanhhà Lại, age 8

A Bird in a Cage

In the back court
next door
a boy spread
cooked rice grains
under a colander
lifted open on one side
by a string.
Brown little birds flew in,
chirping of luck.
I watched the boy grin.
I whispered for the birds
to lift.
But one was slow,
caught inside the trap
when the boy released the
string
and laughed.

Next morning
the bird was set out
to see friends
not confined to
a home-made cage
curved from bamboo strips.
The bird in the cage
sang sad songs.

Next morning
I whispered to the bird
to pretend to be dead
so the boy
would open the cage
and check its warmth.
When the cage door opened
I yelled, FLY.
The bird and I
laughed.

6

[Eric Rohmann]

WHEN I WAS NINE years old, I made a get-well card for my aunt Helen. Using pencil and crayons, I drew her dog, Butchy. The thing is, I had never actually met Butchy except through old photographs. Over years of family gatherings, I had heard stories, always told fondly, of the sweet black-and-white spaniel. To my young mind, I thought that one way to cheer my sick aunt would be to remind her of something she loved. And so I drew Butchy.

I have always made pictures. I drew what was around me, what I liked, and what I cared about. Drawing was how I found my way in the world. That's because drawing requires looking closely, so closely that you begin to see details you'd

by Eric Rohmann, age 9

never see in a glance. You begin to see variations in color and shadow. You begin to see patterns and connections. But as I drew more and more, I discovered something else. Drawing isn't just about seeing. It's about feeling. A picture is not just a description, but a doorway into my thoughts and emotions. A sick aunt, the memory of her beloved dog, a handful of crayons, and the need to tell a story join together on the page.

I don't recall Aunt Helen's response to my card, but many years later, after her death, I found the drawing in a box among her belongings, carefully folded, wrapped in tissue paper with my name written on a yellowed bit of tape.

Eric Rohmann is the award-winning author-illustrator of seven books for children, and in 2004, he won the Caldecott Medal for *My Friend Rabbit*. He was previously awarded a Caldecott Honor for his book *Time Flies*. His other books include the ALA (American Library Association) Notable titles *Clara and Asha*, *A Kitten Tale*, and *Bone Dog*. He has also illustrated many other books—including *Last Song*, based on a poem by James Guthrie, and *Oh, No!*, *Bulldozer's Big Day*, *Bulldozer Helps Out*, and *Giant Squid*, all written by Candace Fleming—and has created book jackets for a number of novels, including *His Dark Materials* by Philip Pullman and *Bless This Mouse* by Lois Lowry. His artwork has been featured in various exhibitions and permanent collections throughout the United States. Visit Eric online at ericrohmann.com.

7

[Linda Sue Park]

WHEN I WAS A KID, I loved reading and writing poems. (I still do.) One of my favorite forms was the limerick. Every limerick I read was either funny or silly. I have a clear memory of wondering why no one ever wrote a *serious* limerick, and I decided to try it.

"Fog by the Ocean" was inspired by the first time I ever saw the ocean. I grew up in Illinois; I was nine years old when my family went on vacation to Massachusetts, including a day at Cape Cod. About a year later, my father bought me a typewriter, and I learned to type. I had a folder full of my handwritten poems, and I typed up the ones I liked best. I loved the way they looked when they were typewritten—much more "professional" than the handwritten versions.

Fog by the Ocean · By Linda Park

On foggy mornings I look out
And boats by the harbor grope about
The fog horn sounds
The ocean waves pounds
On foggy mornings when I look out

Fog by the ocean makes everything grey
As thick clouds on the shoreline lay
The salty sea
On the ocean lea
On foggy mornings that make a grey day.

The herring gulls give the hungry cry
And dive, when dead fish meet their eye
Sea seaweed wash ashore
To waste away, grow no more
And on sandy beaches, here they lie

See through the fog the ocean waves
In which the shell of a crayfish saves
And through gray fog
Tots our collie dog
To smell the salty foggy waves

by Linda Sue Park, age 9

You can also see the beginnings of the fiction writer I would become: We didn't have a dog. But I needed a rhyme for "fog," so I made up the dog!

Linda Sue Park is the author of more than two dozen novels and picture books, including *A Single Shard*, the 2002

<u>Fog by the Ocean</u>

Linda

On foggy mornings I look out
And boats by the harbor grope about.
The fog horn sounds,
The ocean wave pounds,
On foggy mornings when I look out.

Fog by the ocean makes everything grey
As thick clouds on the shoreline lay
The salty sea
On the ocean lea
On foggy mornings that make a grey day.

The herring gulls give the hungry cry
And dive, when dead fish meet their eye.
Sea seaweed wash ashore
To waste away, grow no more,
And on sandy beaches, here they lie.

See through the fog the ocean waves
In which the shell of a crayfish saves
And through the fog
Trots our collie dog
To smell the salty foggy waves.

Newbery Medal winner, and the *New York Times* bestseller *A Long Walk to Water*. Her most recent titles are Wing & Claw, a middle-grade fantasy series, and *Yaks Yak*, a picture book. She has also written two books in the multiplatform series The 39 Clues. Linda Sue knows very well that she will never be able to read every great book ever written, but she keeps trying anyway. Visit her website at lindasuepark.com.

8

[Phyllis Reynolds Naylor]

I **THINK I BECAME** a writer because my parents read aloud to us, almost until we went to high school. It's not that we couldn't read ourselves, and of course we did. But they read with such drama and enthusiasm that family story time—a half hour or more each evening—was my favorite part of growing up, especially my dad's reading of *Tom Sawyer* and *Huckleberry Finn*. Mother also read fairy tales to us, and some were really scary. I think they influenced the first story I ever made up.

When I was in kindergarten, I had a wonderful teacher who sat down on the floor each afternoon and said, "Who wants to make up a story? Come and tell it to me, I'll write it down for you, and you can take it home to show your parents."

I only remember one story I made up, but I do remember the teacher saying, "Phyllis, you've had enough turns for one day; let someone else have a chance."

But here's my first made-up story, which my mother saved.

Once upon a time there was a little boy and a little girl who lived in the woods with their mother. One day the little boy said, "Mother, I want an apple." The mother said, "Okay." The boy reached into the box and the mother closed the lid on him and cut off his head and set him out in the yard and tied a rag around his neck to keep his head on. The little girl came home. She cried a lot. She sneaked out and pasted his head back on with magic paste. Then she put her brother in her boyfriend's house. She grew up and married her boyfriend. The mother died. The end.

As I grew older, my favorite pastime was writing and illustrating little storybooks. These were the Depression years, and we were never allowed to use clean white paper for play, only used paper. My father worked as a salesman for the Heinz company at the time, and my mother worked in the office of a church publishing company. She always brought home a lot of used paper, blank on one side, for me to use for stories.

I wrote about all sorts of things—little books called *Timothy Train*, or another one, *The Food Fairies* (about all the food in a refrigerator going to war). But I also loved drawing lace, so when I started a mystery series, about a beautiful

by Phyllis Reynolds
Naylor, age 10

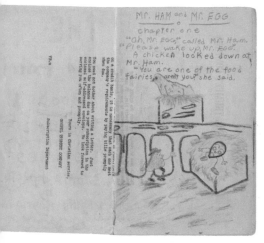

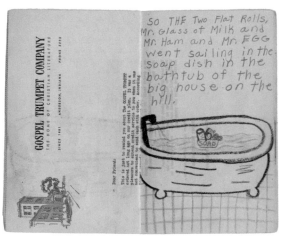

woman detective named Penny, she frequently lost her dress just so I could draw her lacy underwear. Of course, this was usually the point where the boyfriend entered the story, which made it so much more exciting.

When I was sixteen, I received a letter from a former Sunday school teacher, who said she remembered me from her class

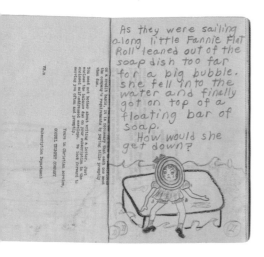

As they were sailing along little Fannie Flat Roll leaned out of the soap dish too far for a big bubble. she fell into the water and finally got on top of a floating bar of soap.

How would she get down?

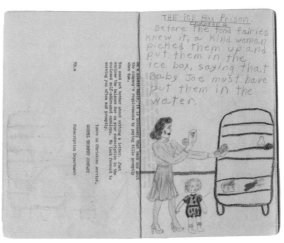

THE ICE Box Prison.
Chapter 6
Before the food fairies knew it, a kind woman picked them up and put them in the ice box, saying that Baby Joe must have put them in the water.

THE Food Fairies wondered how they would get out.

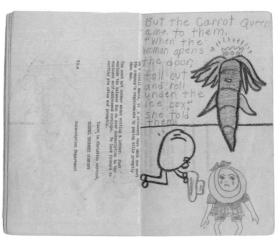

But the Carrot Queen came to them. "When the woman opens the door, fall out and roll under the ice box," she told them.

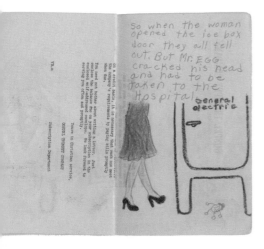

So when the woman opened the ice box door they all fell out. But Mr. EGG cracked his head and had to be taken to the Hospital.

General electric

when they got out of the icebox, King cake and Queen Carrot were crying because they were going to have a war and the enemies had taken Princess Pickle.

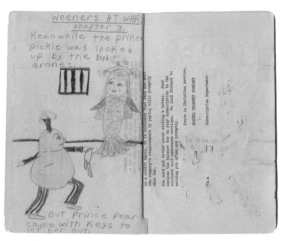

Weeners AT WAR,
chapter 3.
Meanwhile the prince pickle was locked up by the bad drones.

But Prince Pear came with keys to let her out.

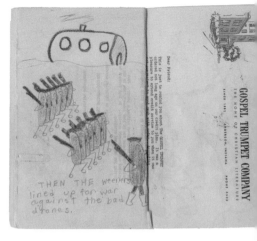

THEN THE weeners lined up for war against the bad drones.

And the weeners chased the naughty drones away and won the war.

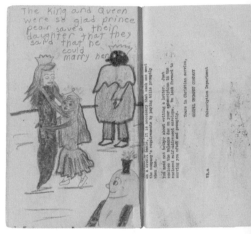

The King and queen were so glad prince pear saved their daughter that they said that he could marry her.

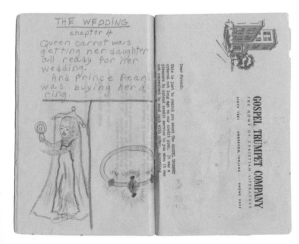

THE WEDDING
chapter 4
Queen carrot was getting her daughter all ready for her wedding.
And Prince Pear was buying her a ring.

So prince Pear took princess pickle to live in the cocoa cup castle. The living room was on the open roof. The castle was beautiful.

and how much I loved stories. She was now the editor of a church paper for children and wondered if I would be interested in writing a story for it. Of course I was, so I wrote *Mike's Hero*, a baseball story, and sent it in. She sent back a check for $4.67. I was so thrilled to be paid for something I wrote, and all through high school, I wrote more and more, learning from editors and trying to make each story better than the one before. In college, I was studying to be a clinical psychologist and was able to pay much of my way by writing and selling stories. When I graduated, I decided I really wanted to be a writer, so I gave up plans for graduate school and began writing full-time.

Phyllis Reynolds Naylor is the author of 145 books, including the Newbery Medal–winning *Shiloh* and the rest of the Shiloh quartet, and the Alice series. She began as a short-story writer and has published approximately two thousand stories, columns, poems, and articles for a variety of magazines and story papers. Her husband, Rex, was her first critic. She has two sons, two daughters-in-law, and four grandchildren, and she lives in Gaithersburg, Maryland. Visit Phyllis online at phyllisnaylor.com.

9

[**Gordon Korman**]

THIS SHOULD HAVE BEEN a lot easier. Find a piece of writing from when I was a kid. That's totally in my wheelhouse. I wrote my first book when I was twelve years old. It was my seventh-grade English project, assigned by a teacher who was actually the track-and-field coach. He gave us total freedom to work on whatever we wanted for the rest of the year. It was February. That added up to a class period per day for more than four months. The result was my first novel, *This Can't Be Happening at Macdonald Hall*—120 pages of bona fide kid writing. I went on to publish four books before I graduated high school, so all that stuff should count too.

But what about *before* seventh grade? That's harder. There

were no computers back then, so none of my old schoolwork was saved electronically. My parents moved a few times, purging a lot of their junk. Except for ancient photos and the hideous trivet I made in Cub Scouts, most of my childhood is gone.

Then I remembered "How to Handle Your Parents." Technically, it wasn't a piece of writing. It was the speech I gave for the fifth-grade public-speaking unit when I was ten. I couldn't find the handwritten original. But my mom—a newspaper columnist—arranged to have it published under her byline back then. She managed to dig the yellowed clipping out of a shoe box somewhere. That's how this middle-grade self-help masterpiece was preserved for future generations.

I can't remember what grade I got on it. It probably wasn't spectacular. Hey, two years later, I only got a B-plus on *This Can't Be Happening at Macdonald Hall*, and that launched a forty-year writing career. Besides, I was a *terrible* public speaker as a kid, shifting my weight nervously from side to side, talking too fast, and laughing at my own jokes more heartily or reliably than the audience ever did.

But here it is, back from the dead—back from the shoe box, anyway—ready to guide millions of kids through the complex labyrinth of dealing with the adults in their lives. Maybe I've been wasting my time writing fiction all these years. Maybe my entire career has been a misstep away from the destiny I set for myself in fifth grade as a self-help guru.

History will decide.

by Gordon Korman, age 10

HOW TO HANDLE YOUR PARENTS

When was the last time you were bawled out by your parents? Probably not much more than a month or so ago. Well, it's a hard life, but we're all in the same boat, trying to row up a waterfall. But luckily, you have me. I have worked out an invaluable system of how to get along with your parents. My advice is absolutely free, although I can't guarantee it. Parents are kind of unpredictable.

Here is a perfect example of what I mean. It's the day after Halloween, and you have eaten enough candy to keep the dentist in business for 25 years. You have a stomachache, and a rash the color of the Canadian flag, and your mother is well into her "I-told-you-so" lecture. The way to handle this situation is to lie there like a rock, look as sick as you possibly can, and by all means, don't open your mouth. If you can convince her that you're dying, she won't take the time and effort to kill you.

Here is another situation you might run into. You come into the house looking like a creature that just crawled out of a swamp. You are so muddy that no one would realize that you lost your pants hours ago. Your shoes—at least the one you have left—well, it's ruined. For some reason, your parents are not interested in the fact that you scored a touchdown. They are hysterical. My advice to you is to pull the "I've got to go to bed! I'm so tired!" routine on them. Seeing as how their happiest time of the day is when you're in bed anyway, they'll be glad to let you go.

Now we come to one of the most deadly situations that you can get caught in. I am referring to the "Clean up your room instantly!" routine. Your room looks like a disaster area. The new wall-to-wall carpeting that you have just acquired is strangely made of Monopoly money. There are books piled all over the place. Somehow, your mother is not thrilled that you read a lot more nowadays. She is holding a book entitled "The Entire History of the World," with the intention of squishing your nose in between the pages. She has also put a siege around your room.

There is no way you get out of this one—not alive, anyway. But you might be able to avoid a very painful experience by hiding behind the biggest pile of junk you can find. If you can hold out until company is coming, SHE'LL clean it up. You may get a couple of dirty looks, but I'm sure you'll pull through.

Well, by now you should have at least a rough idea of various types of problems and their solutions. Good luck. You'll need it. We all do.

Gordon Korman's writing career began when a seventh-grade English assignment turned into his first published novel, *This Can't Be Happening at Macdonald Hall*. Now, four decades later, he is the author of eighty books for kids and teens, most recently *Slacker*, *Jingle*, and the Masterminds series.

He is a full-time writer and speaker, with over thirty million copies of his novels in print in thirty-one languages. Each year, he travels extensively, visiting schools and libraries, bringing his trademark styles of humor and adventure to readers everywhere. You can visit him online at gordonkorman.com.

Gordon Korman, age thirteen, signing the book contract for *This Can't Be Happening at Macdonald Hall*.

10

[Elissa Brent Weissman]

IN THIRD GRADE, all my friends decided they would be authors when they grew up. Naturally, I announced the same. Within a week or two, my friends had chosen different career paths, but not me. I loved to read, and I spent most nights lying across my bedroom floor filling notebooks with novels-in-progress. My favorite books were funny, realistic school stories, so that's what I wrote. One was called *Sisters*, and it was like The Baby-Sitters Club, minus the babysitting. (Perhaps it was also aspirational; I only had brothers.) Another was about a group of kid detectives. Those remained unfinished because the mysteries I created were so mysterious, I could never figure out how to solve them.

My parents bought me a computer when I was ten. Once

I could type my stories, I was unstoppable—and anxious to get my career started. I wanted to be like Gordon Korman, who published his first book when he was thirteen. Actually, I wanted to beat Gordon Korman and be published *before* I turned thirteen. I focused my energy on a novel called *The Ryland Revolt*, about a pair of twins, Sam and Kate, who try to get rid of their substitute teacher. (Where did all these mischievous characters come from? And not liking their teachers? That must have been inspired by books. In fact, I went a little *too* far and took a few things *directly* from books, like the title of my first chapter, which comes straight from a book by Mona Kerby. I didn't invent the trick Kate pulls on her teacher, either; it's strikingly similar to a prank in a book by Barthe DeClements.) My penchant for breaking the rules never went beyond my fiction, though. In real life, I was a goody two-shoes who *loved* her teachers; they did nothing but support and encourage me. One of them, Mrs. Berman, even had me read new chapters of *The Ryland Revolt* aloud to the class each week!

In sixth grade, I submitted the beginning of my novel to ten publishers. I waited, and I planned the sequel, and I rehearsed different ways of announcing my book deal to my class. But it was not to be. Not one company wanted to publish my book. No one even wanted to read beyond the third chapter. It was heartbreaking enough to make me give up on my mischievous twins, but, thankfully, not on writing.

It took twenty years, more hard work, and many, many

more rejections (with some lucky, hard-earned, affirming acceptances along the way), but here I finally am, publishing the first chapter of *The Ryland Revolt*—in a book alongside Gordon Korman.

Elementary-school-Elissa would be pinching herself. Grown-up-real-author-Elissa is, too.

Elissa, age 11, meets Gordon Korman.

Chapter 1.

New School Year Blues

Sam dumped some peanut butter on bread and reached for the jelly. His hand grabbed the pancake syrup instead. Without looking down, he squeezed what he thought was jelly onto the peanut butter and plopped another piece of bread on top of his creation. He dropped the sandwich in a brown paper bag and threw the bag into his back pack. This, and some oreos, a box drink, and a fruit rollup, was his lunch for the first day of school. Mrs. Mayers had wanted Sam and Kate to make their own lunches this year. After all, they were in sixth grade now and she had made their lunches for six years. And now, on the very first day, Sam forgets to make his lunch the night before and ends up giving himself a peanut butter and syrup sandwich.

"Come on!" Kate called from outside. "We're already late!'

"Poopies!" declared Rachie.

"Quiet, Rachie," Sam said as he raced out the door.

Rachie pouted.

"Just come on," Kate told her and pulled her along. "Sam's just got the new school year blues. Now hurry up or you'll be late for your first day of Kindergarten."

Kate was very good with little kids. She thought up all sorts of games and stuff that she didn't mind playing with them. But she also enjoyed Sam, her twin. Of course, she didn't let Sam know. She brushed back her reddish-blonde hair and shifted her back pack to two shoulders. *A back pack is always heavy on the first day,* she thought. "I've got the new school year blues, too," she muttered.

"Not me!" Rachie sang proudly. "No new school year blues for me! Hey, that's a good song. Cha cha cha, no new school year blues! Cha cha cha, no new school year blues! Kate's got 'em! Sam's got 'em! I don't got 'em! Cha cha cha! YEAH!!!! Kate's got 'em! Sam's got 'em! I don't got 'em! Cha cha cha! ONE MORE TIME!!!! Kate's got 'em! Sam's got-"

"I said to be quiet, Rachie!" Sam interrupted. Rachie stuck out her tongue. Rachie was a real pain. She had to be the biggest pest on the face of the earth. She wasn't like most six year olds. She was not shy and *always* said what she thought. Sam was the same way. Actually, Sam and Rachie were exactly alike (except for the fact that Rachie was a girl and was five years younger than Sam). They both had dark blonde hair and green eyes. Pest is a word that you'd use to describe Sam and it was the same with Rachie. But they were both as good as gold and very smart.

Kate was a trouble maker. She, also, shared her opinions, which sometimes were not so pleasant. But she was organized. Organization is a word you'd use to describe Kate. She had had her lunch made the night before, not to mention her back pack packed and her binder totally ready to hold the first assignment in the right section. Some day, Kate would be a famous trumpet player, or actress, or singer, or basketball player, or writer, or composer, or PRESIDENT! She really had a lot going for her because she was very talented.

"All right sixth grade! Watch out! Kate Mayers is here!" Kate declared as they walked up to the front door of their school.

"And her sister Rachie is with her!" Rachie said with her hands over her head. They both waited for Sam to add something. But he was already half way down the hall.

....

" Hey!!!!!! Sam!!!!!! My buddy, my pal! How are 'ya doin'? I haven't seen you in a while!" Slurps, Sam's best friend, called from the other side of the room.

"Yeah, since yesterday, Slurps." In third grade, a new kid called Slurps Slurps instead of Kirk. The name stuck. At first, everyone made of fun of Slurps by calling him that. Now, it was just his name.

"Whatsa matter?" Slurps asked.

"Nothin'" Sam said. "I guess I just have the new school year blues."

Slurps made a face. "Sounds like somethin' Kate would say to Rachie."

Sam pulled the stuff out of his back pack slowly. He was not ready for a new school year. Especially one with Kate in his class. This was not the first time they were together. It had happened once before, in second grade. The teacher realized right away that it was a mistake. Kate and Sam saw to much of each other and started really getting on each others cases. Plus, Kate dragged Sam into every scheme she thought of and got them both in trouble with the principal. He was not sure why they had been put together this year but did not dare ask. His teacher, Ms. Shotter, was the meanest in the school and even Sam would not ask her a question that could be answered with the words, you are a sixth grader and should be able to behave like one.

SLAM!!!!!!!!!!!!!!!!!!!! Twenty- five faces turned to the doorway. That was fifty eyes, fifty ears, and over a million gazillion strands of hair staring at.............. Kate. She was in the doorway, back pack on the floor, panting. She must have dropped her heavy back pack on the floor. Her lips slowly lifted on the sides, her mouth slowly opened, her teeth slowly started to show, and slowly, a big smile appeared. "I've got those new school year blues!!!!!!!" Kate shouted. Sam buried his head.

"Hey, shorty!" Greg Nift knocked Sam's hat off his head. Greg must've weighed 150 pounds. He was about five feet six inches tall and about the same wide. He was the biggest bully in the sixth grade. God forbid someone step on his jacket, and WHAMMO! No teeth! If someone steals the ball from him during a soccer game, WHAMMO! Broken nose! Or even if he's just in a bad mood, WHAMMO! Broken jaw! No one, and I mean *no one* messes with Greg Nift.

"Hi, Greg." Sam said glumly.

"Don't 'hi, Greg' me!"

"Sorry. Can I please have my hat back?"

"No."

Sam took a deep breathe and tried again. "Greg, it's the first day of school. Get in a fight with me later. Please give me my hat back."

A smile appeared on the bully's face, revealing a bunch of black teeth. "No," he said sweetly.

"Children!" Ms. Shotter said sternly. "The bell rang several minutes ago. Get into a seat so we can start."

Sam sat. Greg didn't move a muscle. "Sir, what is your name?" Ms. Shotter asked Greg.

The black teeth appeared again as he answered, "Sam Mayers." Ms. Shotter informed "Sam Mayers" that if he wasn't in a seat by the time she counted to three, he'd be in trouble on the first day of school. She also told him that he was a sixth grader now and should be able to act like one. The famous words of a teacher.

"I'm sorry, uh, ma'am," Kate piped up from the back of the classroom. "But that is not Sam Mayers, it is Greg Nift. Sam Mayers is the boy that is *sitting* next to Greg. I should know. Sam is my brother. Greg stole Sam's hat and wouldn't give it back. I think he should be in trouble."

"Kate-" Sam began.

"Wait a moment. Is this true, *Sam?*" Ms. Shotter questioned.

"Yeah." Sam answered, embarrassed. He wished that Kate would let him handle things himself, in his own way. Kate was always the stronger one. And Kate is a *girl*. It would be embarrassing if your twin sister was stronger than you. If your twin sister was a trouble maker and you were not. If your sister stood up for you instead of you standing up for her. *Kate will be President some day*, Sam thought. And everyone will forget about me. *If I was served double chocolate ice cream instead of triple chocolate......................It's a bird it's a plane............ no, it's Sam's twin sister, Kate! I will save you! Kate will announce. A crowd will gather and throw a party for Kate for saving me from this "horrible crises".* Once again, Kate fought her brother's battles, *the front page of a newspaper will read.* What a wimp Sam Mayers is! Thank goodness for Kate!

"Snap out of it," Kate snapped her fingers in front of her brother's face. "And get a partner. Ms. Shooter wants us to do a project."

Sam shook his head very fast and wiped his eyes as he walked over to Slurps. "Sorry, pal,' Slurps told him. "I already got a partner. You were too busy daydreamin'."

Pete already had a partner and so did Christopher. John was working with Adam and Tyler was moving his chair to Dan's desk. *Darn!* Sam thought. *Everyone has a partner, except.............Kate.* "Oh well, I guess we're together." Kate said to him. "No one else is left, thanks to you!"

"Sorry."

"Hey, it's okay. Come over to my desk. Hurry or we'll be in trouble." Sam brought his chair over to Kate's desk. " We have to protect you from Greg." she said. "You work on the project, a banner that says a school rule on it. I'll make the trap."

"Kate," Sam said. "Stop protecting me! We don't need a trap. Now, just work on the project and neither of us will get in trouble."

"But I know Greg will come over here and torment you," she whined. "I'm making the trap." She immediately started to unlace her shoelaces and pull them out. With the shoelace from the right sneaker, she wove in between her desk and the desk in front of her. In and out, in and out, in and out until it formed a perfect trap. if someone went in-between the two desks, they'd trip. She did the same thing with the desk in back of her, using her left shoelace. When she was finally done, she declared, "No one will annoy you! Not with Kate Mayers as your sister!"

Sam sighed. It *was* a good trap. "Let's just work on the banner."

Their banner was almost done when the classroom phone rang. If Ms. Shotter ever ran, it was to pick up the classroom phone. Unfortunately, her desk was right behind Kate's and she didn't know about the trap. She ran in between Kate's desk and the desk in back of Kate's. Her foot got caught on the piece of string. Waving her arms like a bird wanting to fly, she let out a squawk and went soaring through the air, landing flat on her face with her skirt way over her head. Underwear showing, she just laid there. The class went wild.

Elissa Brent Weissman is an award-winning author of novels for eight- to twelve-year-olds. Her most recent books are sequels to the critically acclaimed *Nerd Camp*, which was named a Best Summer Read for middle graders by the *Washington Post*. *The Short Seller*, about a seventh-grade stock-trading whiz, was a *Girls' Life* "must-read" and was featured on NPR's *Here & Now*. Named one of CBS Baltimore's Best Authors in Maryland, Elissa lives in Baltimore, where she teaches creative writing to children, college students, and adults. Visit her online at ebweissman.com.

11

[Kathi Appelt]

HORSES. I was one of those girls who loved horses. Running horses. Trotting horses. Flying horses. My dreams were all filled up with horses. When I was very small, my only accessibility to them was through the westerns I watched on TV or through the stories that my grandmother read to me, stories like *National Velvet* and *Black Beauty*. But once I began to write, I discovered that I could create my own horses, I could use my pencil to lasso those magnificent creatures and place them on the page. And soon my own stories took up at least some of the space that a real-live horse might have taken, if only . . .

So for me, writing has always been a way to fill spaces,

to explore in a very deep way our most-earnest longings. I couldn't own a horse. But I could create one. And that was almost enough.

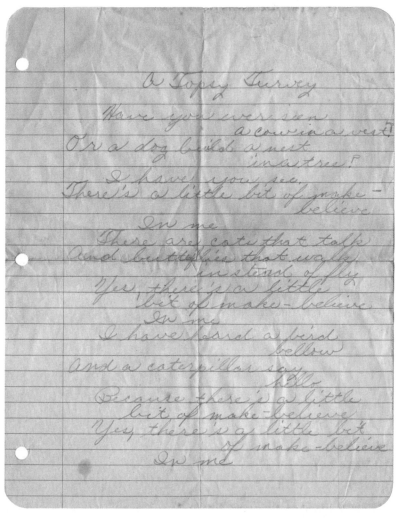

by Kathi Appelt, age 10

A Topsy Turvey

Have you ever seen a cow in a vest?

Or a dog build a nest in a tree?

I have you see.

There's a little bit of make-believe

In me

There are cats that talk

And butterflies that walk instead of fly

Yes, there's a little bit of make-believe

In me

I have heard a bird bellow

and a caterpillar say hello

Because there's a little bit of make-believe

Yes, there's a little bit of make-believe

In me

by Kathi Appelt, age 5

Mrs. Cowgill,
Thought you would like to
know Kathy has worked on
this picture every day since
Monday. She certainly has
shown stick to-it-ness.

Sincerely,
Ann Roach

Kathi Appelt is the *New York Times* bestselling author of more than forty books for children and young adults.

Her first novel, *The Underneath*, was named a National Book Award Finalist, a Newbery Honor Book, and winner of the PEN Center USA Literature for Children Award. That was followed by *Keeper*, which was named an NCTE (National Council of Teachers of English) Notable Children's Book and a School Library Journal Best Book of the Year. Her memoir, *My Father's Summers*, won the Paterson Prize for Young Adult Poetry. Kathi was presented with the A. C. Greene Award by the Friends of Abilene Public Library, which named her a Texas Distinguished Author.

Her novel *The True Blue Scouts of Sugar Man Swamp* was named a National Book Award Finalist and won the Green Earth Award, the Texas Institute of Letters Award, and the Judy Lopez Memorial Award.

In addition to writing, Kathi is on the faculty of the MFA in Writing for Children & Young Adults program at Vermont College of Fine Arts.

She and her husband, Ken, live in College Station, Texas, with five adorable cats: Django, Peach, Mingus, Chica, and Jazz. For more information, check out her website: kathiappelt.com.

JUN 58

12

[Gail Carson Levine]

WHEN I WROTE and published the following story episode in the "newspaper" of the Scribble Scrabble Club, I was ten, the same age I am in the photograph. I'm the shorter girl, standing next to my friend Ruth Hess. I don't have the first chapter of *Adventurous Girls*, and I don't know if there was a third.

It isn't shown here, but the masthead of the newspaper listed the four officers of the club, who were the sum of its members. I was president; Nina Falk, vice president; Ruth Hess (of the photo), treasurer; and—we must have run out of titles—Michael Fishbine, assistant. If I remember right, I didn't keep my position long, because power went to my head, and everyone resented my autocratic ways.

At home, both my older sister and I read, reread, and loved Louisa May Alcott's novels, which are heavy in moral instruction. To our parents' amusement, we became perfect children while we were under the spell of these books, and that must be what I was thinking of in my explanation of the fictional May's good behavior.

I'm glad to see there's character development going on and hints of future conflict, but, alas, no plot yet. This seems to be realistic fiction, although I did love fantasy. Maybe the fantasy would have come too. Possibly the setting that I failed to mention was a castle, or maybe a dragon was going to fly through an open window in the next scene!

Gail Carson Levine writes for children and young adults—novels, picture books, nonfiction, and poetry. She's best known for her novel *Ella Enchanted*, which won a Newbery Honor in 1998 and became a major motion picture in 2004. Other books include her historical novel, *Dave at Night*, and two nonfiction how-to's, *Writing Magic: Creating Stories That Fly* and *Writer to Writer: From Think to Ink*. Her latest novel is *Stolen Magic*, the second in the mystery series that began with *A Tale of Two Castles*, about detective dragon Meenore and ITs assistant, Elodie. Visit Gail online at gailcarsonlevine.com.

ADVENTUROUS GIRLS
by Gail Carson

Chapter II

While the three sisters sleep I will tell you about them.

Judy has blond hair, blue eyes, and is altogether fair. She is 12 years old, and so merry you can't imagine.

I will not tell of Judy's small faults, but I will warn you of her large ones. She is very easy to anger and when she is angry is extremely sarcastic. Once she scared her family out of their wits by being unbearably mean and sarcastic.

Her twin sister, Susie, is altogether different from her except in one aspect, they both L O V E to T E A S E.

Susie has black hair, is dark and is of course, 12, since Judy is her twin.

I will mention one fault of Susie's which is very annoying and also makes a person feel very badly. When in an argument Susie becomes hysterical and is never able to defend herself. Countless times her mother explained that after a trying day most people can't control their emotions any longer, so they use someone in their family as a scapegoat. Once after one of these explanations, Susie burst into tears after her sister made some sarcastic remark. Then her mother didn't know what to do.

The younger sister, May, has brown hair. She is pretty dark. Her age is 10.

May gives the appearance of an angel(really she isn't). The reason for her angelic appearance is that she was reading a series of books about good girl with hardly a fault. I will not mention the fault of May so you will be shocked when she changes. Oh, by the way, the twins did not know the reason for sister's goodness but they noticed the change. I will prove it by telling you what Judy said. "Honestly, Susie, May's been doing something to bring about this angelic fit but I can't seem to find out who or what it is. (to be continued in the next issue)

#
#

by Gail Carson Levine, age 10

13

[Chris Gall]

I HAVE BEEN DRAWING pictures for as long as I can remember. When I was caught doodling on my desk in second grade, my teacher suggested that I might become an artist someday, then made me clean all the desks in the classroom. I really began to find my passion somewhere in the fifth grade. I had tried to draw objects from life, but my trees looked like nuclear explosions. I tried to draw people's faces, but they always looked like zombies. It takes many years of practice to make a drawing look like what it is supposed to be. Instead, I turned to my imagination for inspiration. Fortunately, I had a lot of it, as I was always daydreaming. What would my house look like someday? If I were a mad scientist, what would my laboratory look like? If I traveled the world, how would I get around? Imagining new worlds and places gave me lots of freedom to draw whatever I wanted. It wasn't long before I was studying shading and perspective, and my

Supply

by Chris Gall, age 11

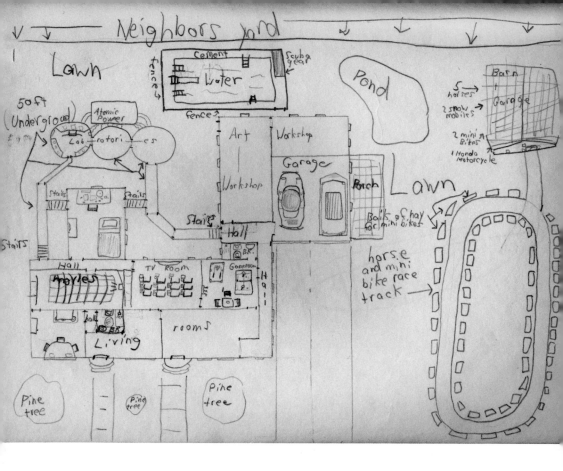

art started to become more realistic. Practice helps a lot!

My drawings at this age suggest that I might have grown up to be an architect or a designer. But really, I was creating new adventures for myself. In seventh grade, I won a READ Magazine Young Writers Award, and that inspired me to create stories to go with my art. My real adventures were just beginning.

Chris Gall is an award-winning, internationally recognized illustrator, and his artwork has been shown in almost every publication in America, including *Time, Newsweek, People, Fortune*, the *New York Times*, and the *Washington Post*.

In 2004, his first picture book, *America the Beautiful*, became a *Publishers Weekly* Best Children's Book of the Year, and his career in children's publishing began. Since then, he has authored and illustrated thirteen more books, including the acclaimed *Dinotrux*, a 2009 *Publishers Weekly* Best Children's Book; *Dog vs. Cat; Revenge of the Dinotrux; Awesome Dawson*; and *Substitute Creacher*. In August 2015, Netflix began airing *Dinotrux*, an animated television series produced by DreamWorks.

Chris has also worked as an adjunct professor of art at the University of Arizona, and he spent four years as a professional stand-up comedian. He currently lives in Tucson, Arizona. Visit him online at chrisgall.com.

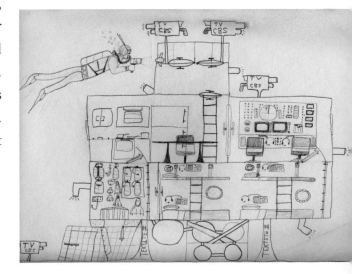

14

[Rita Williams-Garcia]

JACKIE RICE WAS the coolest girl in the sixth grade, which, in our K–6 school, meant she was the coolest girl at Highland Elementary in Seaside, California. Jackie was the first to hit the playground with the newest dances and slang. She was our fastest runner, and in the words of my mother, "That little Rice girl was a taste too grown."

When it was time for our military family to pack up and relocate to Georgia and then finally to New York, Jackie was the first to sign my scrapbook: *To Rita, an off-beat but nice young lady.* My friends were horrified for me and urged me to cross out the "off-beat" part. Jackie's words might have seemed unkind, but I chose to revel in the truthfulness of them. Offbeat. Yes! That's me! And offbeat, I was. Today they call it "nerdy." Still, I was my own brand of nerd. While Jackie brought the latest dances to the playground, I outdanced her. While she was a superb athlete, I was fast, strong, and agile enough to be picked for kickball and dodgeball teams. So, what made me offbeat? For starters, I didn't care about being in the clique of cool girls. Furthermore, I was often under the spell of my own imagination and unashamed to drift off in search of story ideas. I was a daydreamer, reader of the dictionary, explorer of our 1930s Funk & Wagnalls encyclopedia. When homework was done, I was an incessant notebook scribbler.

I kept a lock-and-key diary, but by the seventh grade, I also kept a journal about the daily junior high grind and a sketchbook for story ideas and publishing advice. Most important, I wrote five hundred words nightly—mainly for my elementary school memoir, *Highland*. While the events were true, I couldn't recall the dialogue verbatim, so I did my best to pen the gist of the conversations. I drew the stop sign in the corner of the page to make myself stop writing at one thousand words. I still went over my mark. By the time I finished, on the eve of my thirteenth birthday, I had thirty-nine full notebooks. I had a lot of story ideas queued up in my sketchbook, but I had to capture the Highland years of my faraway childhood home in Seaside while they were fresh. And probably, while I was still that Seaside kid.

By the seventh grade, my reading was all over the place. From Eldridge Cleaver's *Soul on Ice* to Harold

Robbins's *The Carpetbaggers*, Erich Segal's *Love Story*, and more adult books. By the eighth grade, I'd be an Ayn Rand devotee. I was growing up and was reaching for everything.

I had a crush on a trumpet player in band: Franky, the constant subject in my lock-and-key diary. I liked all things "Franky"—including Frank Sinatra. I watched all the Rat Pack caper movies. *Robin and the 7 Hoods. Sergeants 3. Oceans 11.* My obsession with all things Franky inspired my first movie screenplay, written for Frank Sinatra. A down-on-his-luck alcoholic detective takes a dangerous job in Las Vegas to make his alimony payments. I'd even written a Sammy Davis Jr. part. What did this have to do with Franky, trumpet player at Linden Junior High School? Only offbeat, seventh-grade Rita Williams could have made that connection.

In the meantime, I visited the St. Albans Branch Public Library around the corner from our house in Queens, New York, to check out books on the business of writing: *The Writer's Handbook* and *Writer's Market*. I didn't just want to write my stories. I wanted to sell them. I had big plans for the dough that would roll my way. Clothes! Real seventh-grader wear. No more little-girl dresses with Peter Pan collars. And a bra. A real bra that was up to the task at hand. The situation was dire. I had to make money, and writing would be my magic ticket.

I learned how to prepare a manuscript. How to write a query letter. To always include a self-addressed stamped envelope—aka SASE—with every correspondence to ensure an answer. I'd rent my sister's typewriter at five cents a pop, type articles and short stories, and then mail them to *McCall's*, *Ladies' Home Journal*, and *Reader's Digest*. I'd wait four to six weeks. Much to the amusement of my older sibs, a letter of rejection always came sooner than six weeks. Discouraged? Never! I had read that rejection was part of a writer's life. It was official. I was a writer.

Postscript: Alas, Franky the trumpet player and I weren't meant to be. Many decades later, I married Fred, who, in spite of being barred from joining our junior high school band, had made a living as a professional musician. That's another story.

Excerpts from chapters 15 and 16 of *Highland*
by Rita Williams-Garcia, age 11

We went upstairs to the playground which we had to share with Del Rey students. Tention was growing between the two neighboring schools and sooner or later something had to happen.

"Hey Debbie! You brought Stevie."

Debbie Bonner was coming up the stairs with her youngest brother.

"Gee, I hope the teacher doesn't find out or else," I replied.

"Lets play four square," Debbie suggested.

"That won't be easy."

"Why not?" she wanted to know.

"Well," Corazon started, "the Del Rey kids lock the games when we want to play."

"What are you guys doing about it?"

"Believe me, not much," I sighed. "The teachers won't do anything and the Del Rey kids say that its their ball and we're not welcome. I get a feeling that if we go to every four square court on the top playground not one Highlander is playing."

"Yeah?" Debbie had something on her mind. "We are going to play four square."

This was going to be a real showdown. Debbie, Corazon, little Stevie and I walked in step like the Clanton gang facing Wyatt Earp and Doc Holliday at the shoot out at the O.K. corral.

"Get in line and lets see what they're gonna do about it," Debbie ordered.

"Sorry, but the games' locked," a blonde, about Debbie's size spoke up. She was in server's square and from Del Rey, but that was nothing because the whole court was swarming with them.

Debbie didn't move.

Then a girl joined the game and this gave us an opportunity.

"I thought the game was locked," Corazon said.

"We were saving a place for her before the recess," the blonde explained.

"But when a game is locked you can't let no one play no matter what," I cut in. If that girl had any brains she would know that I was bluffing.

"Oh," her tone was sullen.

She fell for it!

"You still can't play," another girl this time a red head replied.

"I can play pretty good," Debbie said.

"That's not what I meant and you know it."

The game tottaly stopped and Debbie stood in the middle of the court. Trouble was about to begin.

"Tell me," Debbie looked the red head straight in the eye, "What did you mean?"

She turned away. "Look, we don't want you and your friends to play, so why don't you just leave."

Debbie took the ball and tossed it to Corazon. Corazon handed it to me.

"Give us back our ball," the blonde demanded, "or I'll go get the teacher. You'll get in trouble for having a little kid on the playground."

"Did you hear what she said? Quote: "Give us back our ball," unquote," I repeated, bouncing it against the ground.

"Number one, it is not your ball. It is Highland property and you are on Highland property. You run to your school, get your own ball, then tell me the game is locked and I'll leave. Number two go get the teacher, I was meaning to talk to her about these segregated courts in the first place." Debbie was good at bluffs and was so convincingly good that they let us play.

I tossed the ball to the blonde in the servers square and we got in line. Before we know it Highlanders came from all over the playground to help us integrate the game.

I enjoyed the music lessons especially during summer school because we had beginners. This would mean the advanced or intermediate section could assist the teacher with the beginners.

We were learning chords. Becky and I took the middle line, the beginners took the top line and Ruby played the bottom. When we put it together it sounded like church music. The kind that you would hear on the late show. Right when they're going to find out who did it.

"Ruby broke her record," Dunya declared. "16 seconds."

"I knew something like this would happen," Becky replied.

"Yeah, give a violinist an inch and they'll take a mile."

"That's that Ruby for you."

Apparently Ruby heard every word we said and enjoyed every minute of it. The 4 feet 4 violinist always found something to smile about and when she wasn't too busy giggling she was off on some dare devil stunt, acting cool and calm having a ball watching everyone's nerves become unglued. That Ruby! So much character in that little body. If I ever get some serious writing done, I'd have to write her in as a character. But her violin playing!

We all seemed to agree on one thing; Mrs. Rote had new methods that teachers were just experimenting with. We picked a subject, discussed it throughoughly with total class involvement, and did further investigation on our own. This month's topic was Soul. The walls and bullitens were breathing gigantic letters of Aretha Franklin, James Brown, The Temptations and Diana Ross and the Supremes. We picked the period right before lunch to work on our soul projects. There was a catch—math and reading assignments had to be completed.

"Debbie, can I cut out a few things from your Ebony Magazine? I ran out of good in my book."

To keep me in suspense, and make me squirm a little, Debbie frowned, looked at her magazine, frowned harder and said, "Wellllll, I'll think about it."

"For how long," I began to get discouraged.

"Now that depends—

"Debbie!" I pleaded. "All I need is a picture of a lady with an afro, come on Debbie."

"All right, but don't let no one outside of Holly and Corazon use it."

"Okay," I looked at her work. "That looks great. Maybe if I added a finishing touch it would—

"And if you added a finishing touch it will be the end!"

"Good bye. I'm going where my art ability is needed."

Mrs. Rote, Debra Anderson and Vivian stapled and pinned up the work while we went on working. I began to get the impression that the guys were getting Black Power and Soul a little bit confused. Eric and Benny Harris drew sketches of clentched fists.

"Hey Rita," Comeal called me from his table, "spell miracles." I could see he was doing a poster on Smokey Robinson and The Miracles. Before I could dictate the first letter Chiefy spelled out "m-i-r-r-i-c-l-e."

"Haha! You're wrong," I always get personal

satisfaction out of doing that loud trumpeter in.

"Let's see you spell it!" he demanded.

"M-I-R-A-C-L-E," I was noted at Highland for endurance writing, a good spelling reputation and was proud of it.

"Let me look it up," Chiefy wasn't satisfied.

"Save your strength, man," Richard came on my side.

By some obvious coincidence, sixth grade students popped in on the other side of the window to view our work. We were flattered, they were envious. In a few days most of our self reservation about Miss Rote began to decrease, shrink and disappear. I mean if you get used to the other sixth graders saying, "hey, too bad I'm not in your class, I wouldn't mind dumping my teaching for a day. All we do is reading, writing and that other stuff."

Rita Williams-Garcia is the *New York Times* bestselling author of nine novels for young adults and middle-grade readers. Her most recent titles are *Gone Crazy in Alabama*, *P.S. Be Eleven*, *One Crazy Summer*, and *Jumped*. She is also the author of two picture books, and her short stories and essays have appeared in numerous anthologies. She is a three-time winner of the Coretta Scott King Author Award and a two-time National Book Award Finalist. Her multiple-award-winning novel *One Crazy Summer* was the recipient of the Scott O'Dell Award for Historical Fiction, a Newbery Honor, and the Parents' Choice Award, and it has been listed on many state reading lists. She was the 2012 Charlotte Zolotow lecturer and the 2015 Virginia Hamilton lecturer. Rita is on the faculty of the MFA in Writing for Children & Young Adults program at Vermont College of Fine Arts, and she resides in Jamaica, Queens, New York, with her husband. Visit her online at ritawg.com.

15

[Cynthia Leitich Smith]

THE WRITER'S DREAM" was the last poem in a collection I wrote during sixth grade.

I spent countless hours in my room, on my canopy bed, pecking away at typewriter keys. I bound the pages with white satin ribbon. I made the front and back covers out of cardboard and heart-dotted red calico.

My goal was to finish in time to enter my school district's competition fair in language arts. Enter I did, though I remember being disappointed at receiving a white participation ribbon rather than a first-, second-, or third-place award.

But I turned one poem into a Christmas card for my parents, and, to this day, my mother keeps it on her desk.

Today, what I notice most about "The Writer's Dream"

The Writer's Dream

I hold dreams of writing

Deep inside my heart.

I want to touch people's emotions

Using this expressive art.

I wish to stimulate contemplation

Of the joy which can partner life,

To diffuse the sorrow of others,

And help them through any strife.

This now shall be my purpose

And a crucially important goal.

For I attempt to return happiness to the spirit

And contentment to the soul.

25.

by Cynthia Leitich Smith, age 11

is that it assumes writing lifts up its audience. That's not true of all writing, but it is true of mine. I've written stories of grief but also healing, monsters but also heroes, of day-to-day challenges overcome through humor and a willingness to keep trying.

And that's what I did as a writer. I kept trying, kept writing, and I'm still writing today.

Cynthia Leitich Smith's first published writing was a "Dear Gabby" column in Mr. Rideout's sixth-grade classroom newsletter. She went on to serve as editor of her junior high and high school newspapers.

Today, Cynthia is the *New York Times* bestselling young adult author of the acclaimed Feral series and Tantalize series. She's also the author of several award-winning children's books, including *Jingle Dancer*, *Rain Is Not My Indian Name*, and *Indian Shoes*.

Cynthia is an enrolled tribal member of the Muscogee (Creek) Nation and was named a Writer of the Year by Wordcraft Circle of Native Writers and Storytellers. She serves on the advisory board of We Need Diverse Books.

Cynthia also is a member of the faculty of the Vermont College of Fine Arts low-residency MFA in Writing for Children & Young Adults program. She makes her home in Austin, Texas. She can be found on the Web at cynthialeitichsmith.com.

16

[Peter Lerangis]

ILEARNED QUICKLY in elementary school that humor was the only way for a kid like me to survive. I was bookish, heavy, really unathletic, and I wore super-thick glasses. For the local shark pit of tough kids, I was the juicy hunk of raw meat. So I stayed clear, and I took comfort in the fact that I could make my classmates laugh. This got me in trouble with teachers. I received four consecutive grades of "U" (for Unsatisfactory) in something called "Self-Control." I never understood that. I thought I controlled myself just fine. It was those other cackling kids who disrupted the class. My habit could be dangerous out of class. If the bullies didn't get one of my jokes, they just made fun of my weight, my sissy habits (you know, like reading), and the way I looked. If they realized the joke was at their expense, they just *altered* the way I looked—in ways that were not very nice.

By sixth grade, I was learning to own my Nerditude. I had become a huge fan of comic books and had developed a fantasy life of my own. I drew a daily comic strip called *Imp*, about a hideous, troublemaking alien who hung out with a Zen-like but clueless middle-aged guy named Oscar Shmultz. Oscar was gullible and simpleminded, but he stayed calm and bemused while everyone around him was going crazy with all the things adults obsess over. He became a hero to me and my friends. We formed an Oscar Shmultz Fan Club. In all things, we asked, "What would Oscar do?" My teachers didn't really get it, or even notice. Except for my sixth-grade teacher, Mr. Shebar. He was the coolest man I ever met. He told me my poems sounded like Bob Dylan. I didn't even know who that was, which made it seem even cooler. He loved to play with words, and so did I. In class, I was free to be as creatively ridiculous or serious as I wanted to be. The red comments on this paper were written by him. I had forgotten all about these two influential men in my life—Shmultz and Shebar—until I found this. And it all rushed back into my brain. With a big CRUNCH.

by Peter Lerangis, age 11

CRUNCH !!

by Peter D. Lerangis

Oscar Shmultz

Will the real Oscar Shmultz please stand up!

Unbelievably, the whole world is set on one word -- CRUNCH! Let me remind you: if there was no crunch where would we be? CRUNCH is used in every day lives. If there were no CRUNCH and we clamped our teeth on food, there wouldn't be any sound. If we stepped on an ant or any other thing or punched someone's nose or even broke a bone and there wasn't any CRUNCH, we wouldn't have a sound to fit the action. Not only that, but if there were no CRUNCH, a candy bar would be without a name. So now you see how much the world depends on CRUNCH. A famous sea captain and his cereal would go nameless and the navy would be inside out as well as the Quaker Oats Co. And Stax. How about Stax? How could it be called the CRUNCH-maker?

Well, just to show you what I mean, let's take a typical American - Oscar Shmultz, and a typical day - April 21.

Now here's the story: You see, April 21 is the day CRUNCH is abandoned from the earth. Now it is the morning of April 21. Oscar Shmultz is ready to eat breakfast. But as he goes down the wooden stairs he hears no CRUNCH! Oh, no! Well, so much for the stairs. Still astonished, he reaches for his only cereal. His favorite - Cap'n Crunch; but, oh, horrors; it isn't there! And it's the only cereal he ever eats! Well, still feeling low, he accidentally falls on his nose. But no sound! Now he's at a point of hysteria! Going to a store, he finds out that there's no such candy as Nestlés CRUNCH! And it's his favorite candy! Oh, this was too much. It put so much pressure and nervous frustrations on Oscar Shmultz and he simply collapsed! And guess what, As he hit the ground he didn't even make a noise.

So next time you hear CRUNCH, never take it for granted.

THE

END

Peter Lerangis is the author of more than 160 books, which have sold more than six million copies and been translated into thirty-three different languages. These include nine *New York Times* bestsellers: *The Colossus Rises, Lost in Babylon, The Tomb of Shadows, The Curse of the King,* and *The Legend of the Rift,* all five books of The Seven Wonders series; *The Sword Thief, The Viper's Nest,* and *Vespers Rising* (the last co-authored with Rick Riordan, Gordon Korman, and Jude Watson) in The 39 Clues series; and *The Dead of Night,* book 3 in The 39 Clues: Cahills vs. Vespers series. His YA novel *Somebody Please Tell Me Who I Am,* co-written with the late Harry Mazer, won ALA's Schneider Family Award and is being adapted into a musical.

Peter is a Harvard graduate with a degree in biochemistry. After college, he became a Broadway musical theater actor. He has run a marathon and gone rock climbing during an earthquake, but not on the same day. He lives in New York City with his wife, musician Tina deVaron, where they raised two sons, Nick and Joe. In his spare time, he likes to eat chocolate. Find out more at peterlerangis.com.

17

[Candace Fleming]

SOMETIME around fifth grade, I started keeping journals, spiral notebooks that I filled with lists of words, ideas, and descriptions. I made up characters, tried my hand at writing song lyrics, and chronicled my day. ("Lynda and I went for pizza. Mike Drake is cute.") There were also dozens of stories begun and abandoned. Time and again, I wrote a beginning, sometimes a middle, and then . . . nothing. I would move on to a new idea. Try on a different story.

As an eleven-year-old, I lived in the world of books. I devoured mysteries and fantasies and historical fiction. Like my favorite authors, I wanted to write stories that would leave my readers feeling all wild and trembly inside. But I didn't know how. So I imitated the authors I loved. After reading *Anne of Green Gables*, I filled nine pages with the start of my own orphan story. When I read *The Murder at the Vicarage*, I tried my hand at writing a British mystery: "Cotsworth Manor was in an uproar. Someone had put poison in Lady Agatha's tea."

I titled this piece *Who Done It*. As usual, it fizzled toward the middle, the story unfinished, the mystery left unsolved. Still, I thought it needed a gold medal. All the best stories had one, right? And so I pried off the Newbery sticker from the class copy of *The Witch of Blackbird Pond* and stuck it on the first page of my story. It dazzled, so gold and shiny . . . until my teacher, Mrs. Gaskill, made me put it back.

I now know I was developing my ear. Through reading and imitating (and even pilfering other people's Newbery Awards), I was learning about good writing. I was practicing my craft. And maybe . . . just maybe . . . I was waiting for a story (and maybe even an award) of my very own.

One winter's day, my father came home with a chess set. He set it up at the dining room table. "Black or white?" he asked. I sat down at the black side. I'd never played before. I soon discovered that chess was . . . well . . . like a story. Knights and kings outmaneuvering each other, battling it out, trying to capture each other's queens. It was all so dramatic.

That night, I wrote about chess. It came out this way: "When Sir Bauer arrived at the tower deep in the forest, it had long been abandoned." I remember sitting back and rereading that

CONTINUED ON PAGE 109

by Candace Fleming, age 11

The First Move

When Sir Bauer arrived at the tower, deep in the forest, it had long been abandoned. It stood alone, a small rough stone tower, overgrown with moss and gray lichens. A spring bubbled steadily in the darkness at the base of the steep circular staircase that led to the small room at the top of the tower.

Sir Bauer observed the tower for sometime before pushing open the heavy iron door that stood slightly ajar. Pidgeons flapped wildly from their nests, and the dank air slapped Sir Bauer in the face. The room he entered into was littered with twigs and feathers, and there were signs that other knights before him had stayed here also.

The black queen had recieved word that the white army had invaded her territory, so to be sure Sir Bauer was sent out as scout for her majesty. He had traveled over the black territory with his black labrador retriever keeping a lookout for the white army. So far no sign of the white army had been found and so sir Bauer decided, after fourty eight hours without sleep, to rest. After a good nights sleep he would return to her royal highness and report his firdings.

Meanwhile in the Black queens ummer palace, in the dark timbered ll th   were clustered in groups feverishly talking about the news that had just arrived. Silk

The Black queen dressed in crimson and black velvet heavily embrodied with black pearls, paced the floor of her chamber with clenched fists, her eyes flashing and her black hair swirling.

"War they want, and war they shall have! How dare they invade my royal dominoin!"

"My dear," the warlock of night said "We must look to our defenses and see that they are in good order."

"I have already sent the page out to give Sir Bauer my orders. He is to guard the Black castle and the tower in the woods," the queen said quite unexpectedly.

"I am sure," the Black warlock said confiendently, "That the black army shall win victoriously over the white army. The magic and unearthly forces are with us, they are at our command. We shall surely win."

The Black queen leaned back into a black velvet chair and smiled, for this was the kind of talk she liked.

Sir Bauer meanwhile had slept until evening not wanting to meet up with the Black queen and have to explain why he didn't obey his orders and pursue the white knights. He was now wide awake and after a snack of bread and cheese he set out cautiously into the forest. Hours later he reached a

clear patch of ground. The trees were
farther apart and the fog was dispensing
letting the moonlight flood the field.
White birches stood straight and silvery.
Sir Bauer looked at the trees, How uncanny
they looked. They didn't have anything
like this in the kingdom of the night.
Terrified he muttered a spell against evil
and realize he had ridden into the enemys white
kingdom, the kindom of day. He turned
and began to retreat when out of the
white firs came a man richly dressed in
flowing white robes. He was a white bishop
of the white queens palace. Had Sir
Bauer known this he wouldn't have
approached him because the bishop of
day was supposed to have as much or
more unearthly power as the warlock of
night.
The bishop of day rudely aroused
took up yelling for help as Sir Bauer
rode up sword in hand. The bishop
ingnored his orders of surrender and
continued his screams until Sir Bauer,
much alarmed silenced him with a cut
of his sword.
More shouts were heard and
Sir Bauer realized that he had wandered
into an enemy camp. His only escape
would be the white mule for his
steed could no longer carry him
quickly to the outskirts of the camp.
He jumped on the mule and gave it

a switch of his sword. The reluctant beast gave way to a gallop and heading straight toward the sounds of the enemy. Sir Bauer as hard as he tried could not control the beast and as he headed for a large white tent Sir Bauer braced himself. The mule came to a sudden stop and Sir Bauer flew over his head and landed upon a battle axe left by one of the white queens guards, killing himself instantly on the sharp edge of the axe.

And so the first move was made by the black knight capturing a white bishop and getting captured in return.

"The First Move" won this first-place blue ribbon in the Coles County (Illinois) Creative Writing Contest.

sentence, running my fingers over the letters. And I remember being struck with a sudden and surprising thought: *Huh, that's pretty good.*

So I kept going.

I wrote all the way to the end.

Candace Fleming is the prolific and versatile author of more than thirty books for children, including *Muncha! Muncha! Muncha!*, *Boxes for Katje*, *The Fabled Fourth Graders of Aesop Elementary School*, *Clever Jack Takes the Cake*, and *Oh, No!*—all of which were named Notable Books by the American Library Association. Her nonfiction titles include *The Lincolns: A Scrapbook Look at Abraham and Mary*, which won the 2009 *Boston Globe–Horn Book* Award for Nonfiction; *The Great and Only Barnum: The Tremendous, Stupendous Life of Showman P. T. Barnum*, winner of a 2010 Award for Excellence in Nonfiction for Young Adults; *Amelia Lost: The Life and Disappearance of Amelia Earhart*, a *New York Times* Notable Book; and *The Family Romanov*, winner of the 2015 *Boston Globe–Horn Book* Award, the *Los Angeles Times* Literary Book Prize, the NCTE (National Council of Teachers of English) Orbis Pictus Award, and a Sibert Honor. Candace is the 2014 recipient of the Children's Book Guild of Washington DC's Nonfiction Award, given for her "substantial body of consistently high quality nonfiction books for children of different ages." She lives in Chicago, Illinois. Visit her online at candacefleming.com.

18

[Brian Selznick]

THE STORY IN MY FAMILY is this: My grandmother's maid gave me tinfoil to keep me out of trouble. I'd use it to sculpt things like flowers and dinosaurs. According to the lore, this was my introduction to art. I've drawn and made things ever since. In kindergarten, I remember getting a lot of attention when we all had to draw a seal with a ball on its nose and mine was the best. My kindergarten teacher wrote on my report card, *Brian is a good artist.*

I grew up in East Brunswick, New Jersey, and was very lucky because there was a really good art program in the schools. My teachers Mr. Jones, Ms. Feder, and Mr. and Mrs. Koppel were all very important to me. I also took art classes after school with Eileen Sutton. I was her student from around fifth grade until I graduated high school about seven years later. I learned so much from her, and we're still in touch. The first thing she taught me was to put a little white highlight in people's eyes. It's the little white highlight that really brings the face to life. I think of her every time I put a little white highlight in people's eyes.

By the time I was ten years old, I'd discovered the art of Leonardo da Vinci and Michelangelo and other artists from the Renaissance. I'd copy their work from books for hours. My favorite painting was *Madonna of the Rocks* by Da Vinci. The angel's sublime face was a particular favorite. I began to experiment with crosshatching (building up the image with lots and lots of little lines that cross back and forth). I still use crosshatching when I draw.

Angels were fun to draw, but so were monsters. I found a magazine called *Omni* when I was eleven, which in the 1970s published articles about science and sci-fi. On the cover was a painting of a strange creature by the artist H. R. Giger, who went on to design the monsters in the movie *Alien*. I became really obsessed with his scary artwork and created my own monsters, inspired by his use of skeletons and horns.

Around this time, the original *Star Wars* was released, and after I saw the movie, I drew all my favorite characters. I'm not sure why I picked Grand Moff Tarkin to draw. I also drew more popular characters like Princess Leia and Darth Vader, but I guess Grand Moff Tarkin made an impression too. (You'll

In the drawing: "Selznick", "Da Vinci study for angel in madonna of the Rock"

by **Brian Selznick**, age 10

notice I spelled his name wrong!) I'm probably the only person in the world who has ever drawn a picture of Grand Moff Tarkin when they were eleven. Also, I must have done this drawing before I met my art teacher Eileen Sutton because there is no little white highlight in his eyes.

Brian Selznick is the author and illustrator of many books, including *The Invention of Hugo Cabret*, winner of the Caldecott Medal and the basis for the Oscar-winning movie *Hugo*. His other books include *Wonderstruck* and *The Marvels*, as well as *Amelia and Eleanor Go for a Ride*, written by Pam Muñoz Ryan, and *The Dinosaurs of Waterhouse Hawkins*, written by Barbara Kerley, which received a Caldecott Honor. He also illustrated *Frindle* by Andrew Clements as well as the first three Doll People books by Ann M. Martin and Laura Godwin, among others. He lives with his husband, Dr. David Serlin, and they divide their time between San Diego, California, and Brooklyn, New York. Connect online at theinventionofhugocabret.com.

by Brian Selznick, age 11

GRAND MOFF TARKEN

19

[Tom Angleberger]

I BETTER PREPARE YOU for what you're about
to read.

Imagine another world. The world of Yodium. A
world of swords and sorcery, thrills and adventure!

Now . . . imagine a series of encyclopedia entries about
that world!

You're still not ready because I need to add one more
thing: These are intensely boring encyclopedia entries from a
really badly written encyclopedia!

Instead of swords and sorcery, we get stuff like this: "This
government, of 15 elected officials, decide on any important
issues."

Or how about this from the entry on the country of Lifad:

"Of course, it has many ship builders so people can ship grain and cattle."

And this is all just chapter 1. I guess I never wrote chapter 2, but thanks to some notes in section 7, we know that it would have included "the, many, more details" on the country of Ganila, including a section on "the Mongolian Swamp."

Why did I write bad encyclopedia entries when I was a kid? I guess for the same reason that I wrote bad comics, bad comic books, bad poems, bad jokes, and the start of a bad novel: Basically, I never shut up. I was either talking, writing, or yammering away inside my own brain.

In the many years since then, I still haven't learned how to shut up. But I have learned something: Whether you're talking or writing, you can't just blah blah blah all the time. You've got to think about who is listening and figure out how to keep them listening and how to make what you're saying sensible to them.

There's a difference between *story* and *storytelling*. There might have been an interesting *story* behind Yodium, but I buried it under terrible *storytelling*. If you'd like to try to dig it out, you can try. But feel free to skim past the grain, the shipbuilding, and especially the fifteen elected officials.

by Tom Angleberger, age 12

north
Pole

western
hemisphere

5

4

N f2 3

south
pole

Yodium,

Is a Planet in one
of the recently discovered planes
of Mongol. It has 7 continents
Lifon, Swide, Myn, Plithia, Gamila, Lyindup,
Findis. As you could see It is
mainly ocean, but it also has
some large continents such
as Lifon, And some totally civilized
governments such as the government
Gamila. The rest of this chapter
talks about each Country, All 10

1
Lypina

This country depends mainly on agriculture. They grow mostly wheat and other grains, though they also have many ship building businesses, especially on the north, west cost.[*1]

The Government of this country is one of the best. The capitol is Ni Oigo,[*2] from here this government, of 15 elected officals, decide on any important issaes. Mass Al= LG Gov= LG (Formoz)

2
Nastonia

Nastonia is basicly like Lypina except for its government.

Nastonia and Lypina are almost constantly at war.[*3] Nastonia has a government that is an absoulute Tyranny. Mass Al= NG Gov= CE

At this moment Lypina is winning the war.......

*1 marked on map by 🏴
*2 " " " N
*3 Place war is at now is marked by ♦

3

Unirio this country is covered mostly by deserts, and is not capable of sustaining much life, in fact the only known human life is on the border of Mastonia and is ruled by Nastonia.

This country was a perfect democracy until Nastonia's army took it over. There is a rumor that YDIM is on the way. MassAI=NG GOV=CE

4

(Formerly Vodac) now Mynarh
this country used to be controled by an Evil King. But...

This great group consisting of Mynarh (the Paladin)(Kraksion (The organizer and Justice of Gurily and a Fighter magic user An Acrobat and a thief who have not released thier names

Y D I M

Has struck.....
The evil tyrang in this country is gone, the great YDIM has Attacked the castle And taken the Country.

✓ A

Now this country is ruled by
Kralien. Ydim* came in and
took control of this country. Now *1
this country is Just like Gainila

5 Lifad

This countrye takes up most
of Lifen. It has a fairly
democratic government and its
main source of economy is ranching
and growing grain. Of course it
has many ship builders so
people can ship grain and cattle
Not much else is known about
this country.

6 Syfiña

This country has remained
nuetral in the war its nieshbors *2
are having. It has always stayed
very aloof and has built a great
wall around its border, with no gates.
Nothing else is known

* see chapter 2 for more about Ydim
*1 see Gainila
*2 see Ydim and #2

7
Ganila

(See chapter 2 for the, Many, more details about Ganila)

This country is organized by kratien, It is mostly self-supported. Ydim is based in this country and takes it's orders from kratien

(Don't miss chapter 2's section on The Mongolian swamp)

8 a
Lyindup -
and
8 b
- Platra

This is a very strange assituation because Lyindup and Platra are on two different continents they are still one country.

They are a bit more toward totalicianism than democracy but they aren't that bad atall.

9 ?
This is not a country but an area forbidden to be entered

✓

for some reason The surrounding
countries religions have forbidden
anyone from going in, Some rumors
say that There are some people
living in that country, and sooner
or later YDIM will investigate.

10 Swide

        Swide is a Truly awful
place. IT's laws are much
like out Communism, except for
The Corrupt, scummy Villians
sure To be found anywhere, YDIM
will probably hit This place
soon.

        Y D IM is basicly
Trying To clean up This place,
And they are doing a good Job.

        This world is, as I said,
In the largest of the planes
of Mongol (Water, swamp, land).
        Due To the time period all
This Takes place, Travel is limited
except for YDIM and a few others
who have Talented Wizards.

Chapter 2 next week

Tom Angleberger is the author of the *New York Times* bestselling Origami Yoda series, as well as the Qwikpick Papers trilogy, *Fake Mustache*, and *Horton Halfpott*. A former newspaper reporter, he teamed up with other former reporters to cowrite the time-travel adventure *Stonewall Hinkleman and the Battle of Bull Run* and the science-fiction thriller *Fuzzy*. He also frequently collaborates with his wife, author-illustrator Cece Bell, most recently for the easy reader series Inspector Flytrap. Currently, he is writing and illustrating a series based on the Marvel superheroes Rocket and Groot. Visit Tom online at origamiyoda.com.

20

[Alex Gino]

AS A KID, I was determined to write a book. I still have a folder full of world-building first chapters and mostly empty charts to track my progress through writing the rest of the story. No plots to speak of, though, which is still my biggest challenge as a writer: *Okay, so I've got these cool people with an interesting life situation . . . but what do they actually* do?

I had written away for information on vanity presses, before self-publishing on the Internet was a thing, and I pored over the booklet that explained how, for a fee, they could turn your story into a real-live book. They would even design a cover for you. Of course, I didn't really want to pay them. I would send my book out to "real" publishers first (once it was done, or at least more than one chapter long), but it was good to know I had a backup.

A Background of the Future is the book I wanted to send out on submission, the fact that it is only one chapter long notwithstanding. In this draft that I share with you, I was typing my full contact information on every page, like it said to do in the booklet. There are several versions in my folder, as I added details and "perfected" the story. (I put "perfected" in quotes because I've since learned that "perfect" isn't actually a word that describes writing. As much as the perfectionist in me hates it, there is always a matter of style and preference, and while writing may be astounding, or gripping, or gut-droppingly life-changing, it's never actually "perfect." Okay, enough with the writing lesson. Moving on.)

I hope you find my twelve-year-old white kid from New York City views of 2035 as seen from 1990 half as hilarious as I do: MODEMS and modern slang, my theories on education, and my own notion of an invented, international language. And if you're only about twelve yourself and half the references don't make sense, just trust me: The Doomsday Clock was a thing, and everyone in the eighties was named Jennifer.

by Alex Gino, age 12

CHAPTER 1: A BACKGROUND OF THE FUTURE

My name is Alexandria Kelly *7. The *7 in my name is used
to classify people even more nowadays, since there are a lot of
people in this galaxy in the year 2035.

My brother's name is Mark, a very common name.

I am 12 years old, and I am in the 65th level at school.
By the way, there are 100 levels of school to equal what finishing
high school used to be. All of these levels are taught on
computers. I am smart for my age, and taught never to be humble,
ever, as you might notice in this book.

My brother Mark,8, is in the 10th level. Can you believe
it? He'll be in school until he's 25 because the levels get
harder as you go along. Levels 95-100 can sometimes take 6 months
to a year just to complete one. He probably will not go to the
extra-special levels, (like what college used to be), from levels
101-500-something, but more are constantly being made. You
choose different levels depending on what you want to study.
I'll probably major in science and become achemist. I'd love
to discover a new element.

Anyway, Ithink that if you read this book, you are going
to need to know the meaning of certain words in slang. Hotto, fresh,
uncommon-like, well-liked, in, and coolo all mean something
that you like, or you enjoy, or something that is in style.
Cold, spoiled, common-liked, out, and stratchy all mean something you hate do not enjoy, or something that is not in style.
Minor means very small, and colonel (don't ask why) means
very large. Contractions are used constantly by many people.

-1-

Pez dud (another question not to ask) means hello, an seya,

(pronounced sēyă), which is still another word not to ask the

origin of, means goodbye. I'll probably use these words a lot

in my book.

In case you don't know, this is a book written in 2035

to go back to the year 1990 if a time machine is ever invented.

I personally think that a time machine is possible. I am not

the only one. If it ever happened, it would be hotto.

Another thing that you should know, is that I live on

the earth. My mother and father saw that too many people

were going to the moon, so they decided not to go. They decided

to stay here, where they thought they could get more and better

land, instead. I think differently though. I think that living

on the earth's moon would be fresh.

Although Mark, my parents and I live on the earth, my

best friend, Jennifer Smith and her family will start their

trip there in three days, on Friday. Can you believe it?

Oh, by the way, Jennifer is related to Mikhail Gorbachev, the

great Russian leader who turned the Soviet Union into a democracy.

Its new official name is the United Soviet Democratic Republic,

the U.S.D.R. for short. Off the track again. I always do that.

Anyway, Jennifer and I are devastated. We've tried everything

possible to stay together, but our parents are stubborn. She

says she'll write every other week, and I said I'd write on the

other weeks, but I'm not so sure.

The Inter-Galaxy Postal Service brings mail from the earth

to its moon and back every other week, and one of us should

have a letter on it.

-2-

Gino

Staten Island, NY
10303
·(718)

Now a rocketship a week supplies and other things, (including mail), to and from the earth's moon may semm like it would cost a lot of money, but the price of launcing a rocketship has lessened a lot.

My parents are called by their first names by everyone, which are Robin and John. This is a common thing to do. John is a very common name. Robin is pretty common too. That is why my parents named me Alexandria, a not so common name.

This book is a special assignment my computer disk for level 64 said would be good for me to do, and I thought it was well-liked, even though nobody in the past would probably read it.

In case people in the past read this book and want to know, scientists, and I agree with them, do not think that there is life anywhere in the galaxy besides the earth and its single moon.

I think that it is important for you to know about language in 2035. The official language is a mixture of all of the languages existing as of 2028, but most people just use the language they grew up with. They teach the language, its called Zeus (after the Greek god), but most people don't speak it except into their computer. I try to practice Zeus everyday, but my brother never tries to learn it. Until the year 2070, disks for your subjects will be made in Zeus and all other languages, but after that, they will only be made in Zeus. Also, Juno (after the Roman god) is the official money currency, with an important document to prevent things like inflation.... This now stops some problems in trade and will, in the future,

Gino

Staten Island, NY
                10303
(718)

stop many problems in communication. I thought the idea was
in, but an old lady (just under 90 years old) thinks the idea
is what she calls "unhip", whatever that means.

In case you think that Majorie (the lady I just told you
about) is old, I think I should tell you that the average

◯

life span for a female is 97, and the average life span for a
male is 95. This is because spoiled diseases like pnumonia
and AIDS either have cures or medication to control the effects
of the disease. Even some types of colds have remedies. Isn't
modern science great?

You may or may not have heard of the doomsday clock. It
uses one hour for a scale. Zero minutes is practically a nuclear
war, and one hour is no possible chance of a nuclear war.
Right now I think that the doomsdayclock is at about 20 minutes
from doomsday. The relationship between the U.S and the U.S.D.R.
is building and getting better. Many people think the time
until doomsday will keep on rising and that doomsday will
never come, but who knows. Anything's possible.

Anyway, I think that this is enough infomation to get you
started. If you have any problems, or you don't understand
something, just call 1-58-55456-6164738921/71524859301/17845981.
Don't worry. You don't have to use all of these numbers at once.
The "1" is for the earth. The "58" is for the U.S.. The
"55456" is the area code. The "6164738921" is for if you're
using a fax machine. The "71524859301" is for if you're using
either a regular telephone or a visual telephone. The "17845981"
is for if you're using MODEM on you're computer. MODEM hooks
you're computer up with other computers. Isn't that fresh?

Anyway, on with the future.

Alex Gino loves glitter, ice cream, gardening, awe-ful puns, and stories that reflect the diversity and complexity of being alive. Born and raised on Staten Island, New York, Alex has lived in Philadelphia, Brooklyn, Astoria (Queens), western Massachusetts, and Oakland, California. They will take a quiet coffee date with a friend over a loud and crowded party any day. Alex is honored and delighted to be able to write for young people who are starting on the path of figuring out who they are and how they want to be in the world.

Alex's Stonewall Award–winning debut, *George*, received four starred reviews and is currently being translated into twelve other languages. Alex's second middle-grade novel, an evolving work-in-progress, is set to be an intersectional tale about best friends, baby sisters, first crushes, and racist, ableist police violence. You can reach Alex through their website at alexgino.com.

21

[Tim Federle]

WHEN I WAS TWELVE years old, I was a completely average student with one above-average ambition: to be on Broadway. Other daydreamers had their heads in the clouds. I had my head in Times Square—inspired by a touring production of *Cats* that I saw in third grade and never forgot. The following piece was written as a sixth-grade diary when I went away to my first sleepaway camp in the Poconos (I grew up in Pittsburgh), where kids got to choose either an "arts" major or a "sports" emphasis (guess which one I chose). Camp lasted three weeks—an eternity, it seemed, before I got there, since I'd never been away from home before—but one audition for *Annie* later, it all worked out. (Or, most of it, anyway, if you didn't eat the food.)

I ought to note here that I'd never kept a diary before those wonderful, eternal weeks in the mountains, but my mom had the good sense to know: (1) that I loved gifts, so sending me away with a brand-new journal felt cool simply because it was "brand" and "new"; and (2) that twelve is a really good age to start reflecting on your life and figuring stuff out. I treasure this written record of that time in my life, because, frankly, I felt like such an outsider that to read these pages again reminds me that I was adorably normal in a lot of ways. I only wish I'd never stopped journaling. If nothing else, it's really good source material when I need to get back into the headspace of the only-slightly-shorter-than-I-am-now version of me.

"Farewell Island Lake"
Camp Diary
by Tim Federle, age 12

Sunday, August 9

Today was my first day at Island Lake Camp. It seems cool. Everyone seems pretty nice. I think for my schedule I'll do:

Acting Workshop
MINOR
Horseback Riding
MINOR
MINOR
Cartooning.

The food isn't great, but it's good for camp. I might try some magic or circus. There's so much that it seems overwhelming. I'm already a bit homesick but I'll be OK. Mom sent me presents which was comforting. The room isn't that good, but it's only for 3 weeks. I better go to bed now.

See ya,
Tim

WHAT A DAY TODAY WAS!

First I auditioned for "Annie," the camp musical. Then I went to cartooning, and then to horseback riding, where I learned all about the danger of the sport.

Next I went to "the trapeze." I was scared to death and wasn't fabulous, but what an experience! Then I went to magic class—and was impressed.

About "Annie"—I'm the male lead; the part is Daddy Warbucks. My *NEW SCHEDULE* is:

1. "Annie" rehearsal
2. "Annie" rehearsal
3. Horseback riding
4. ANYTHING I WANT
5. ANYTHING I WANT
6. Acting improv class

It's a lot different than my old schedule, but it's better (in my opinion).

Well, off to read the comics.

See ya, Tim

Tuesday, August 11

I finally got my new schedule. Today, I first went to "Annie" rehearsal. It was fun but I think I have to wear a bald cap!

From there, I went to the "Challenge Course." It was so fun but so scary!

A 40-foot tree had pegs running up the side that we had to climb up. At the 30-foot mark we get off onto a cable, with two ropes above it, which you held onto.

At least I had a safety cord on.

I better go and memorize my lines, now!

Bye, Tim

Wednesday the 12th

Today was another "great."

At "Challenge Course," I climbed 30 feet and then climbed across a wire with a wire 2 to 4 feet above it (Example A, below).

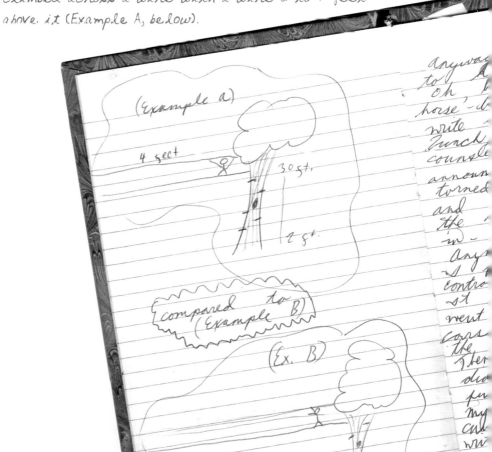

At least we were strapped in.

Anyway, from there I went to horse-back riding.

Oh, before I write about horse-backing I have to write something else . . .

At lunch, when the head counselor went to make announcements, ANOTHER counselor (Dave Morgan) turned CONGO music on and we all danced to the lake where we jumped in-in all of our clothes!

Anyway, at horse-back riding, I felt a lot more in control than the first time.

Well, better leave 'cause my hand hurts and my head can't think of anything to write.

Chow now,
Tim

Thursday, Aug. 13

Today was a good day. In the morning I went to "Annie" rehearsal where we practiced a new scene in which I first meet "Annie."

I stayed to practice more after.

Next was lunch, which I won't say anything about. Tomorrow I will compete in a horse-back competition against another camp. At dinner, we had some OK Chinese food.

Later on tonight, I asked Dory, the girl playing Annie, if she'd go out with me. She said, "Yes," so after camp ends I'm going to keep in touch. So as you can see today was GREAT!!!!

BYE, TIM

Friday, August 14th

I won second place today in a horse competition (I just learned how to trot a day ago!).

I didn't do much more today except for rehearsal (we staged the New York scene) and had a boring improv class.

Tonight, though, I talked to Dory + Leah (Dory and my friend) and that was a lot of fun.

Tomorrow, I'm seeing a movie with her.

Well gotta go!
Tim

Saturday, August 15th

It was Lazy Day at camp today.

We saw the movie "A League of Their Own" which was very good. We got to sleep in today till 10:45 and then got to have a great lunch.

Tonight I hung out with Dory. Nothing much more happened.

Gotta go,
Tim

Sunday, August 16th

Dory dumped me because she felt "funny" being in the same production. So, I feel angry but I guess I better be nice to her. Everything else was boring and I'm pretty mad.

Better go,
Tim

Tuesday, August 18

Sorry I didn't write yesterday. Today I got to finally call my mom and dad to say Hi!

First I had a very boring rehearsal and then another. Then came an OK lunch (the dessert was good). Next, I went to horseback where I learned how to Post while Trotting.

IT WAS FUN!

Dinner was actually pretty good (considering that it was a peanut butter and jelly sandwich).

In improv today we talked about the relationship with the director (of anything that has to do with the theatre).

Anyway, at the evening activity, COLOR WAR broke out. The lights went out and then they held up a sign saying, "COLOR WAR `92" and then they told us the team names: LOONEY TUNES and DISNEY!

Thank the Lord I'm on Disney!

COLOR WAR is between two teams and each has a color (I'm blue) and we compete in warrior events.

See ya,
Tim

August 22 1992

Wow!

It's been awhile since I've written. Disney won COLOR WAR.

Horseback riding was fun today. We learned how to lunge. I went to CHALLENGE COURSE (again, example A).

It seemed boring this time.

I also went to swimming which felt great-today was about 73 degrees.

"Annie" rehearsal is A LOT more intense.

Adios
(I hope that's how you spell that),
Tim

Sunday, August 23

Today was a <u>very good day</u>!

"Annie" rehearsal went smoothly.

Horseback riding was great because the instructor said that I was the only one who listened.

It was so hot, though, that I changed my "minor" to water-front (instead of calligraphy) and cooled off.

I finished my day with an interesting improv class where I became a hippy named Moonbeam.

Well, better go-
Tim, '92

Monday, August 26

Lately I've been a bit homesick but I'm OK.

Yesterday I dove into water that was too shallow. I lightly hit my head but my back hurt so Sharon, the water counselor, took me to the infirmary.

EVERYTHING IS OK.

Anyway, I'll be home soon and off to school . . .

AAH!

Bye,
Tim

Saturday, August 29

Well farewell Island Lake Camp!

What a time I've had. Today I packed and said goodbye. It was one of the saddest days I've ever had.

Tonight I went to banquet where we were served GOOD food. No, really, I'm NOT lying.

Anyway, then they had a big sign of "Island Lake" being burned in the middle of the lake on a float. We all sang "That's What Friends Are For" and then hugged goodbye.

Well, that's it for camp life. What a great time I had; between "Annie" and horseback, waterfront and the challenge course, Island Lake camp will remain with me forever.

Goodbye, summer '92, hello school.

OH NO!

Till next,
Tim

Five foot seven and afraid of the dark, **Tim Federle** is, against all odds, an adult. His debut novel, *Better Nate Than Ever*, was named a *New York Times* Notable Children's Book of the Year, and the book's sequel, *Five, Six, Seven, Nate!*, won the Lambda Literary Award. Additionally, Tim co-wrote the Broadway musical adaptation of *Tuck Everlasting*. Say hi online at timfederle.com.

22

[Kwame Alexander]

THIS WAS MY FIRST "real" poem. My mother still has the same frame in her living room. (I spent most of my paycheck as a busboy on that frame. Back then, minimum wage was $3.35 per hour.) What I lacked in actual craft and skill, I certainly made up for in confidence. It took me two days to construct this epistolary poem, because it was my first poem and I wanted it to be perfect and I kept starting and stopping and trashing and the wastebasket in my room was overflowing with drafts and I'd get discouraged and eventually it kinda gelled and all the while I found it quite fun to be in control of the words in that way. When I finished, I just knew I was the next Langston Hughes. My mother cried when she read it, and I remember saying to myself, *Wow, words are powerful!*

I love you, Mommy
you are so special to me
Ever since that day in '68
when you brought me into this world

I could have made this poem rhyme, but
that means I would have had to really
think
When I'm with you, I shouldn't have
to think
My feelings for you are deep,
but unhidden

What can I say?
I've been with you for nearly fourteen years
I've loved it and
I'm sure you have
I couldn't and wouldn't have made it
this far without you
You are the best mother in the world and
I love you

Well mommy, there is not that much else
to say
except that in me, every day is
Mother's Day.

by Kwame Alexander, age 13

Kwame Alexander is a poet, educator, and *New York Times* bestselling author of twenty-one books, including *Surf's Up*, *Booked*, and *The Crossover*, which received the 2015 Newbery Medal, the Coretta Scott King Author Honor, the NCTE (National Council of Teachers of English) Charlotte Huck Honor, the Lee Bennett Hopkins Poetry Award, and the Paterson Poetry Prize. His other works include the award-winning children's picture book *Acoustic Rooster and His Barnyard Band*, recently optioned as a children's television show, and the Junior Library Guild Selection *He Said, She Said*, a young adult novel.

Kwame believes that poetry can change the world, and he uses it to inspire and empower young people through his Page to Stage Writing Workshop, which has created more than seven thousand student authors at seventy-six schools across the United States, Canada, and the Caribbean. A regular speaker and workshop presenter at conferences in the United States, he also travels the world planting seeds of literary love (Brazil, Italy, France, and Turkey). Recently, Kwame led a delegation of twenty writers and activists to Ghana, where they delivered books, built a library, and provided literacy professional development to three hundred teachers as a part of LEAP (Literacy, Empowerment & Action Project) for Ghana, an international literacy program he cofounded. In 2015, Kwame served as Bank Street College of Education Center for Children's Literature's inaugural Dorothy Carter Writer-in-Residence. The Kwame Alexander Papers, a collection of his writings, correspondence, and other professional and personal documents, is held at the George Washington University's Gelman Library. Visit him at kwamealexander.com.

23

[Grace Lin]

IN MY NOVEL *The Year of the Dog*, the main character, Pacy, writes and illustrates a book and sends it to a national book contest. She wins fourth place and $400; and that win cements her dream of becoming an author and illustrator.

This is a mostly true story (in fact, the whole novel is 97 percent true). In middle school, I really did enter a national book contest and I did win fourth place. However, in *The Year of the Dog*, I claim that the book Pacy wrote is *The Ugly Vegetables*. While I did write and illustrate *The Ugly Vegetables* (it was, in fact, my first published book), I made that book when I was an adult and I never entered it into a contest. The book I really did make in middle school, the book I really did send to the contest, is this one!

And this one is titled *Dandelion Story*. It began as a social studies project where students were asked to imagine a civilization based on a religion (which I think we picked out of a hat). I chose Taoism and found inspiration for my imagined civilization from my science fair project—an experiment I called "The Plants' Taste Test." I had grown five to six different bean plants, feeding each with a different liquid—orange juice, milk, soda, etc. Each plant reacted differently, which made me imagine that plants had their own preferences and tastes—just like people. So, it was an easy jump (for me) to imagine a Taoist-inspired civilization of flowers.

Little did I know that, years later, I would be reading old Taoist tales as inspiration for my own books (like the "Knowing the Fish" story in *The Year of the Rat*). And that my own books would be read and shared with hundreds and thousands of kids who were the same age I was when I wrote *Dandelion Story*. In fact, so many students have read *The Year of the Dog* that they often ask me if I'll ever publish that first book. I've always said "No," as I don't think it was that good. But, at least now you can get a peek at it!

You might be a little surprised by what you see. I was trying very hard to be a serious writer, and, back then, I thought being serious meant being sad or miserable. So, my very sullen author photo was my attempt to look serious. And (spoiler!) the dandelion in the story dies in the end. That's one of the reasons why I don't think it's that good now. Nowadays, I would rather have my work make people feel happy or inspired or grateful instead of depressed! But, maybe, seeing part of my old work might still make you smile (or laugh)—so that would be good too! Enjoy!

Dandelion Story

written and illustrated
by
grace lin

by Grace Lin, age 13

PROLOGUE

If one day you decided to take a walk in a forest and you were lucky, you might be walking in a very special forest. And if you were very lucky, you might reach the exact center of that special forest. And if you were that extremely lucky person, then you would be amazed at what you saw.

There would be almost a wall of trees- tall and elegant, enclosing a circle. Many have mistakenly thought that human hands have created this perfect arrangement, but that is not so. The mad wind has shaped the branches and trunks around the magic place within.

You would see the wild, climbing roses and vines twisting around the trunks and blocking your view of the inside. But if you were very, very lucky, you might be able to find a thinner part of the dense vines and brush some of the aroma-filled flowers aside and peer through.

And if you could peer through, you would be overwhelmed by the mystic beauty that filled you. You would feel a mysterious emotion in your chest- like a silk ribbon unwinding.

And you would see a garden, not really a garden, but an array of flowers and vines and leaves. Each single blossom with a certain poignancy, a certain delicacy. Each flower in its full bloom and radiant color. The roses, the forget-me-nots, the lilies, the daffodils, peonies, daisies and violets- all grouped together and twisted in a breathtaking arrangement.

No, it's not the Garden of Eden or the lost hanging gardens of Babylon. It is Verdance. A place of green and vibrant colors, a place of flowers and beauty.

So you would look, and you would not talk or move or even breathe. And you would listen. To hear the movement of the swaying flowers, to hear a falling petal. And if you listened carefully, you would hear more then that, much more. Stop, and I will tell you what you hear.

"The golden sun touches the peak of the mountains and seems so far way, " said the daffodil,"Yet, I feel its warmth so strongly on my blossom."

"It is a beautiful sunrise,"said the forget-me-not.

And the rest of the flowers gave murmurs of agreement.

It was silent for a moment, all intaking the brilliance of the sun and feeling the rays on their leaves and stems.

"Why does the sun come out every morning?" the rose asked itself, "Is the sun the moon with it's blossom open? Or are they two different flowers?"

"Are they flowers at all?" the lilac chimed in.

And again a silence came, a silence for questions.

"I think the sun is a flower," said the tulip, "perhaps a bursting red and orange peony."

The peony bended slightly.

"Perhaps it is the heart of the rose, when the petals are pushed away," said the lily.

Again a silence. A silence for thoughts.

"I wish the sun would come here,"said the violet wistfully, it is always behind the trees."

"Yes, to have it move like the wind. To have it come and go," said the daisy.

And a silence followed again. A silence for wishes. A silence for dreams.

    "I.." began the marigold, but stopped   as   the   wind
arrived.

    "Hello," the wind whispered.
    The flowers bent slightly as the wind talked.
    "Hello,"the flowers said politely.
    "Tell us,"said the marigold,"You have traveled
everywhere?"
    "Yes," whispered the wind.
    "Then, tell us," said the Queen Ann's lace, "Have
you seen the sun?"

"Yes,"the wind whispered, "Many do not wish to get too close to it."

"Why?" the day lily asked.

The wind blew and softly touched the flowers.

"Flowers," the wind whispered, "I have seen men building stone buildings, animals in cages, flowers-like you-being potted and planted in straight lines and cut to a certain shape. Men, people-following certain guidelines and rules. They whisper about laws and do not dare not to follow them."

The flowers bowed their heads and many drew back, horrified and scared.

"Rules? Laws?" asked the peony in confusion.

"They prohibit you,"whispered the wind, "Some places do not allow you to dream and think."

The flowers made no sound.

"But, at the same time," whispered the wind,"I have seen a palace of shining stones- sparkling and glittering in the radiance of your sun. Bold colored jewels and luminous pearls strung and hanging on one woman's neck. I have seen dark, curling smoke rise in the air and slowly disappear into the sky. A child smiling in its sleep, delicate and rosy. I have seen people renewed with hope and glory and love. And I have seen the sun. Yes, I have seen the sun."

   "Take me to see the sun," a dandelion said, "Take
me to see the sun, the palace, the men. I want to see
them. I want to see the colored jewels and smoke. I
want to see them all!"

   The wind circled the small plant.

   "Do you really want to?" whispered the wind.

   "Yes, "the dandelion said.

   The wind hesitated, then whispered, "I could bring
you."

   "Then take me to see it," begged the dandelion,
"Take me now."

The wind whispered,"You wish to go so badly. I would have to pull you from your roots. You may die."

"It would be worth it. To experience it, to see what I can only hear and dream of here. I want to see the sun. I want to know what it really is," the dandelion said, intoxicated with the images and ideas.

The wind again circled the plant. And carefully, slowly grasped the dandelion, ripping the roots from the soil. The other flowers winced at the imagined pain, but the dandelion made no sound.

The dandelion rose, higher and higher- over the perfectly arranged trees and branches. Over the vines and leaves. And then into the sky and clouds. It was then the dandelion noticed something.

"You can see the clouds all around you and besides you, yet when you get to where they are, they are still ahead of you. And when you reach to touch them, they aren't there," the dandelion said.

"Yes," the wind whispered.

"Why?" asked the dandelion.

"Dreams are made of clouds,"whispered the wind, "They aren't meant to be touched or held. They are clouds. They are dreams."

The dandelion was silent.

The wind traveled over countryside and rivers. The dandelion saw glimpses of fish jumping in streams and animals running in forests. Suddenly the wind slowed. And the dandelion was in human civilization.

6

Grace Lin is the author and illustrator of picture books, early readers, and middle-grade novels. Grace's novel *Where the Mountain Meets the Moon* was a 2010 Newbery Honor Book, and *When the Sea Turned to Silver* was a 2016 National Book Award Finalist; both were *New York Times* bestsellers. *Ling & Ting*, Grace's first early reader, was awarded the Geisel Honor in 2011. Recognized by the White House as a Champion of Change for AAPI Art and Storytelling, Grace most often writes about the Asian American experience in her books because she believes, "Books erase bias, they make the uncommon everyday, and the mundane exotic. A book makes all cultures universal." See more about Grace and her work at gracelin.com.

24

[Chris Grabenstein]

I FIRST STARTED having fun writing when I went into the comic-book publishing business in the fifth grade.

I'd pass around my mimeographed copies of *Super Dooper Man,* my friends would laugh, and I was hooked. Writing was fun. A way to be cool that didn't involve athletic skills or good looks, neither of which I possessed.

By sixth grade, I was writing skits for my friends to perform in our annual school talent shows.

In seventh grade, I was a big fan of Art Buchwald, who wrote funny essays in the Sunday newspaper. So, I decided to write my homework assignments the same way. Fortunately, I had an English teacher with a sense of humor. She wrote in the margins of my composition book: *You will make your living as a writer some day.*

When your parents say nice things about you, you figure that's their job. But when a teacher tells you something, you actually believe it might be true.

As you will see in the sample from my eighth-grade composition book, where the teacher asked us to write the classic "What Do You Want to Be When You Grow Up?" essay, by the age of thirteen, I had decided I wanted to be a writer or a

by **Chris Grabenstein**, age 13

English 8 Composition

Chris Grabenstein

September 1968 - June 1969

Signal Mountain Jr. High

Signal Mountain Tennessee

To Be or not To BE

"Here, Chicky, chick, chick", I murmered
as I tinkered with my newly
acquired "Farmer Brown Farm kit".
At that time to be a farmer was my goal.
        Well, time passed on and between
Dr. Kildare and Ben Casey, my
new idles, the image of being a
doctor occurred in my mind. From
that time on, 'no matter if it was
~~the~~ army or cowboys and Indians,
I was the one with the "Little
Doctor Dopey" sets. With the candy
pills, plastic sorenges, and spoons
for scapels I might have been
able to do a transplant.
        But now my mind wanders
to a new thought. To be a
~~comedian~~ comedian or a
writer is my quest.
              If this "flops", I would
be content to be a millionare
and run Grabensteins Department
Stores if I could ever fit the
name on a sign.

B+

comedian. From that point on, all my focus went into trying to become the best writer I could be. Unfortunately, I sort of went overboard. I asked for a thesaurus for my birthday. I asked for a dictionary for Christmas. I used them both with reckless abandon. Here is an excerpt from another eighth-grade essay I recently rediscovered in an antique spiral-bound notebook (I didn't want to torture you with the whole thing):

October 25, 1968
Autumn is the time of trekking
down the cold-nipped street,
looking in tranquility at the majestic splendor
of the landscape laid out
in front of you like a silk linen cloth.

Yes, I am using big words.

No, they are not, necessarily, the right big words.

I still don't know what a cold-nipped street might be. Maybe the cold was so frigid, it nipped off the asphalt's edges?

I do know now that linen and silk are two different kinds of cloth, so you can't really have a "silk linen cloth," unless, I guess, you're a worm that ate too much flax. So much for the "majestic splendor" of the landscape laid out in front of me.

And why was I looking in tranquility? Was I enjoying autumn at Tranquility Base on the moon?

Unfortunately, when I was in eighth grade, I was sort of showing off. I had not yet learned one of the most important rules of writing, as spelled out by the great Elmore Leonard: If it sounds like writing, rewrite it.

But, I was having fun with words.

And guess what?

I still am!

LIONS HONOR THRASHER STUDENT—Chris Grabenstein, student at Thrasher Elementary School, accepts the first-place essay award from Dr. Arch Smith, president of the Signal Mountain Lions Club, which sponsored the Citizenship Essay Contest for the fifth and sixth grades at the school. Left to right are Ralph James, principal; Mrs. W. L. Nason, fifth grade teacher; the essay contest winner; James T. Smith, chairman of the club's citizenship and patriotism committee, and Dr. Smith.—(Sttaff photo by George Moody.)

Chris Grabenstein receiving his first writing award in fifth grade.

The Quakers

The Quakers were most holy Folk
Who on Sunday did not tell a Joke
They knelt and they prayed
There memory is saved
On an old cardboard box of their oats

The Pilgrims

The pilgrims came over on a boat
They ate rich turkey and goat
They drank and wrote
Their stomachs did bloat
For there was no Pepto Bismol afloat

Paul Revere

There was an old man named Revere
Whose horse was his one greatest fear
When he witnessed the light
He ran off in fright
And screamed that the redcoats were near

Mr. Draco

There was an old man named Draco
Who wanted to fly to Quako
He searched and he sought
But no plane could be bought
So he got it from his empty box of Flako

A

Chris Grabenstein is the author of many fast-paced and fun page-turners, including the *New York Times* bestsellers *The Island of Dr. Libris*, *Escape from Mr. Lemoncello's Library*, *Mr. Lemoncello's Library Olympics*, and *Welcome to Wonderland: Home Sweet Motel*. Nominated for forty different state book awards, the first Mr. Lemoncello book has spent over one hundred and five weeks in the top ten of the *New York Times* middle-grade bestseller list and will be a Nickelodeon movie. Chris is also the co-author with James Patterson of the number-one bestselling I Funny, Treasure Hunters, and House of Robots series. You can visit him at chrisgrabenstein.com.

25

[Yuyi Morales]

I **DON'T HAVE** many pictures of me at the age I made this painting. Just the year before, I had entered the new world of middle school, and already I had transformed from a disciplined kid with good grades into someone rather invisible, except for the times when teachers called my name and I didn't know the answers to their questions.

In those days, I went through many changes; I cut off most of my long child hair and I let my fingernails grow. I wanted to feel like I was already a señorita, a young woman, but I was only twelve and my body was responding slowly.

On the first day of school, we, new students, were received by a short, sturdy woman with a golden cap on her front teeth; we were told to call her Prefecta. Standing at the front of the classroom, Prefecta shouted the rules of our new middle school student's life. We were not children anymore, she announced; we now were future delinquents. It was her job to catch us in all kinds of corrupt acts to make sure that we respected school and to hopefully straighten up our wrong ways. The consequences are unthinkable, she scolded. We had better be very, very afraid of anything we could do.

Señor Cruz Mata was next. Our math teacher shuffled his octogenarian feet toward the chalkboard and, without uttering a word, began writing numbers and formulas I had never before seen in my life. There was a rumor that Señor Cruz Mata had suffered a stroke that left him moving with difficulty and speaking with a mumble. But Señor Cruz Mata was still good at pointing with his cane and ministering judgment. Right away, he parted the class between the good students and the bad students. Those who knew what he had written on the chalkboard were the deserving kids. A group of about five students sitting at the front smiled. The rest of us . . . well, we were doomed. Teacher after teacher, and day after day, I began recognizing the evidence of my lack of talent as a student, and I accepted my destiny. I was *tonta*, dumb. My teachers knew it, and now I knew it too.

No more effort on my part was necessary from then on; after all, stupidity and no talent show whether you try or not.

From the window of my classroom, while trying hard not to try, I could sometimes see the next year's students at a class called Artisticas (art). This was quite a distracting sight. The class took place outside in the school yard—how unusual! There was a lot of brown paper involved, and wire, and other materials I couldn't see very well from my desk, but what I *could* see was the slow growth of papier-mâché figures way bigger than the kids that were building them. What was going on? Week after week, I saw the teacher and the students outside making what I could only imagine were incredible things. I could not wait to be in the next grade!

And one day, I was.

I don't remember the name of my teacher, but he was a lean man of brown skin, wavy silver hair, and a well-trimmed mustache. His sleeves were always rolled up. Some of his first exercises were to teach us how to draw straight lines in our notebook. He instructed us in how to move our arm completely from one side to the other while tracing the line, no stopping or making tiny connected lines, but one long, uninterrupted line instead. I still use what I learned in that first lesson; even though I often erase and redraw them, nowadays my drawn lines are mostly firm and continuous.

But I was a bad student, right? Bad students are not supposed to have talent, or fire, or to distinguish themselves for doing well, so I couldn't just go and suddenly be good at this. Actually, as the school year progressed, I could not even make myself ask questions or tell my teacher that I dreamed about being part of the small group of kids he would choose to build the giant brown paper sculptures. I was a failing student. How could I even dare to be more than that?

One day, it was time for our final project. We were going to make a painting!

I don't remember at all how I got a framed piece of canvas and the paints or the brush I needed; up to that point in middle school, I had not been good at telling my mother about the supplies or the books my teachers asked us to buy for class (a main reason why I kept turning in incomplete assignments). But what I remember extremely well were the instructions that our teacher gave. Your painting, he said, should be a creation of your own imagination. "Do not copy from anywhere! Make something of your own."

That was going to be a difficult task to accomplish! Something of our own. . . . Well, I loved drawing, and the things I liked drawing the most were people and animals (in many of my first drawings from when I was a little child, some of which my mother kept, the papers were covered with drawings of little girls, like me, sporting fabulous hairdos and accompanied by dogs). For my class, I decided I was going to make a scene with a baby. I knew I could handle a human image because I had had a lot of practice drawing faces, including my own. I also decided to have the baby be surrounded by animals. First, a cat, and if I drew him curled up, sleeping and showing only his back, I could figure it without copying from anywhere. And what about my favorite animal? Yes, I would include a dog, a huge dog! But, wait. What do real dogs look like? I knew they had noses and ears and snouts and more, but, really, could I draw what they look like only from my memory? I agonized a lot about what I did next.

I went to the encyclopedia my mother had bought us years before and looked for a photograph I remembered seeing of the face of a Saint Bernard dog. My teacher had been so clear about not copying from anywhere, so I decided to study this image with my eyes, and I traced invisible lines with my finger around the shapes of the dog's face. I did this again and again until I thought I could remember most of the picture, then I closed the book and went to my painting to try to re-create from memory what I had seen.

The result is this painting you see here. I remember feeling proud of the result—for I had never done a painting before in my life—but I also remember feeling worried. Had I cheated? When I tried to re-create the photograph from the encyclo-pedia after being told not to copy, had I finally become the delinquent I had been so much warned I could be?

My teacher looked at my painting. Then he looked at me. We were standing outside by the plant's bed on the school patio, where the class was taking place that day. "You copied this," he said. I lowered my head. I wanted to say something, but words refused to come out. Could I really explain what I had done with the encyclopedia? And if I said that I didn't copy, was it true? I could only manage to shake my head

LARINO

by Yuyi Morales, age 13

without even looking up. "No?" he asked. "Then someone else made it for you."

He gave me the next-lowest grade short of failing. I stood there for a long time after he was gone.

Many, many years passed before I knew art was my life. Nowadays, when I look at this painting, I fantasize about how awesome it would be to time travel and make a visit to my young self, still standing there holding this embarrassing painting in her hands. I would come over, and, of course, she wouldn't know who I am. As she is standing there trying hard to hold in her tears, I would lean by her shoulder and whisper in her ear, "Yuyi, you just keep it up and draw more, and yes, copy, and wait, because you won't believe the things you'll do one day."

Yuyi Morales was born in Xalapa, Mexico, the city of flowers and springs. After migrating to the United States in 1994, she struggled with English and loneliness in a culture foreign to her but found solace in public libraries, where she read children's books with her son and discovered a renewed interest in stories and art. She is now the author and illustrator of many books for children, including *Niño Wrestles the World* and the *New York Times* bestseller *Thunder Boy Jr.*, and is a five-time winner of the Pura Belpré Award for an outstanding work of literature for children that best portrays, affirms, and celebrates the Latino cultural experience. Other honors include the Américas Award, the Golden Kite Award, the Christopher Award, the Jane Addams Award, and the Tomás Rivera Award. In 2015, she received the Caldecott Honor for her book *Viva Frida*. Visit her online at yuyimorales.com.

26

[Ashley Bryan]

I **WAS BORN** in New York City in July 1923. My earliest memories are of my drawing, drawing, drawing. After my earliest drawings, under ten, I copied comics and art from magazines. To free myself from copying, I began drawing from life, using my brothers and sisters as models. The enclosed drawings are from 1938–1939. I was in high school, fifteen to sixteen years old, graduated at sixteen. These drawings are the source that nourished my growth as an artist.

Love   *Ashley*

by Ashley Bryan, ages 15–16

1938

Ashley Bryan grew up to the sound of his mother singing from morning to night, and he has shared the joy of song with children ever since. A beloved illustrator, he has been the recipient of the Coretta Scott King–Virginia Hamilton Lifetime Achievement Award and the Laura Ingalls Wilder Award; he has also been a May Hill Arbuthnot lecturer, a Coretta Scott King Award winner, a Newbery Honor winner, and the recipient of countless other awards and recognitions. His books include *Freedom Over Me*; *Sail Away*; *Beautiful Blackbird*; *Beat the Story-Drum, Pum Pum*; *Let It Shine*; *Ashley Bryan's Book of Puppets*; *and What a Wonderful World*. He lives in Islesford, one of the Cranberry Isles off the coast of Maine.

(your photo here)

The next
story is yours.
How will it
begin?

Here are some tips from this book to get you started:

⭐ Read, read, read

⭐ Draw, draw, draw

⭐ Listen to stories

⭐ Daydream, doodle, and let your imagination run wild

⭐ Use words and pictures to express your thoughts, dreams, and emotions

⭐ Get inspired by authors and artists you admire (like the ones in this book!)

⭐ Practice, wait, and revise-you'll get better and better if you stick with it . . .

⭐ But remember that no writing or art can be "perfect"

⭐ Believe, as R. J. Palacio says, that "an artist or writer is just about the greatest thing a person can become in life, the highest kind of achievement"

⭐ Have fun!

Like many of the people in this book, Elissa Brent Weissman has been writing stories since the time she could hold a pencil. Now grown up, she's the award-winning author of five novels for young readers, including *The Short Seller*, *Nerd Camp*, and *Nerd Camp 2.0*. Visit her online at ebweissman.com.

Born

Grave

Jarrett Krueger

Corona

rock

C
N